DAVID BOYD

NORMAN NICHOLSON
A LITERARY LIFE

To Bob J.
with very best
wishes from
David Boyd

First published in 2015 by
David Boyd

A CIP Catalogue of this book is available from
the British Library

ISBN: 978-0-9928261-0-9

Typeset in Bembo 11pt by
www.chandlerbookdesign.co.uk

Printed in Great Britain by
Berforts Information Press

Acknowledgements

I simply cannot allow this book to see the light of day without some mentions with immense thanks to a whole brigade of people who have helped me in so many ways. Many, such as the Walthamstow Hall schoolgirls who found themselves evacuated along with 'Miss Garnier' in charge to deepest Shropshire over seventy years ago, have so generously and helpfully passed on to me their memories. It has been both immensely useful and a great privilege indeed to have been able to access so many extant personal memories of Norman Nicholson and of his quite vast and closely-woven web of contacts. Others have given of their valuable time in practical support; yet more have tendered motivational first aid when things - as they do - went rather wrong.

With trepidation, for I shall inevitably be forgetful and make omissions, I'd like particularly to thank: The Norman Nicholson Society and especially Peggy Troll, Dr. Antoinette Fawcett, Prof. Alan Beattie and Charles

Lambert thereof; Professor Barry Spurr and especially Mr Bernard Hamilton for kind and generous help regarding George Every; Professor Andrew Gibson for all his encouragement as well as scholarly guidance; Professor Marjorie Perloff for the generous academic recommendation and for permission to print it; Margaret Hunt for much help about the religious drama; The London Library for invaluable research material; The University of Manchester John Rylands Library (Fran Baker especially); Cumbria County Archives; Susan Harrison for putting-up with my endless revisions; The Open University for first igniting my burning interest in modern poetry many years ago; Millom Parish Church for the front cover image of their Norman Nicholson Window; Rebecca Wood for allowing use on the back cover of her striking picture of Norman Nicholson; Canon Dr.Vincent Strudwick for his kind help regarding his time at Kelham with George Every; James Critchley of Merlin Media for the ace cover artwork; John and Frances Chandler at Chandler Book Design; C.R. Mittal; Grevel Lindop; Diana Manister; Justice Alan Wilson...... the list goes on and on, and extends globally.......

All the above and many more have helped to make this book possible: conversely, there have inevitably been a few who have been less than helpful or occasionally even obstructive but it would be unseemly and inappropriate to dwell upon that topic, in this particular context: anyhow, perhaps some if not all of the difficulties were caused by my own actions or omissions in approaching them.

Needless to say, I take complete responsibility for anything which is at all wrong or inaccurate within the pages of this book, and I'd be pleased to receive any corrections etc. c/o the publishers.

Seascale, Cumbria
April, 2015

“This book is dedicated to Judith,
for everything, really.”

CONTENTS

Introduction

The Whispering Poet was the title of a 1972 BBC TV *Look Stranger* series documentary film about Norman Nicholson. This choice of title aptly reflected his characteristically quiet, yet urgent, *'Psst! – listen to me! - I want to show you something!'* mode of communication, and the title together with its accompanying images perhaps hinted at the nature of this rather solitary yet singular character's life in and around this decaying post-industrial small town on the outer fringes of the county then named Cumberland.[1] But the whole film contained little or no indication of the very broad scope and the sheer quality of Nicholson's literary output, nor did it question the rather paltry critical recognition its subject's works had received. The many contradictions and complexities of Nicholson's personal life and character were similarly not made very apparent in the film.

'The best Poet Laureate that Britain never had' might perhaps have been a more appropriate title, but no single

phrase, however pithy, can hope to sum it all up. That, rather, is the overall aim of this critical biography of Norman Nicholson, English Poet (1914–1987).

A biographical subject's life and critical study of that subject's *oeuvre* usually each demand differing approaches. It is sometimes proclaimed that literature should be approached with disregard for the author's biographical details but, in Nicholson's case especially, his life events and their particular locations positively shaped his literary works.

For example, had he not contracted tuberculosis as a teenager, Nicholson's life would almost certainly have taken a very different path: probably one leading far away from the town of his birth. His literary works, if any, very probably would have taken on a very different form and content. Similarly, had he not been deprived of his natural mother when aged only four, his emotional, social, and perceptual development would almost certainly have resulted in the formation, from infancy onwards, of a very different human being to the one Nicholson ultimately became.

In a local radio interview[2] towards the end of his life, Nicholson explained that, unlike others with the opportunity to fall back upon an alternative means of earning a living, as a young but very disabled adult he had had absolutely no option but to persevere in his efforts to become a writer, in spite of years of rejections and rebuffs – experiences which would have forced better-placed or healthier individuals simply to give up trying.

Despite coming from a rather ordinary family background, Nicholson was intellectually extraordinarily gifted. His habitat of Millom was the absolute antithesis of, say, Bloomsbury. Millom's tough, grimy ore miners and ironworkers must have regarded this strange person in their midst as a very peculiar interloper. Yet Nicholson felt a need to stay put in the town of his birth for nearly all of his seventy-three years of mortal life, to remain part of the community which inhabited this isolated place. He loved to roam Millom's rural hinterland, making both town and country and their respective flora and fauna the focus of his attention and the inspiration for his writings. Perhaps with a nod to Wordsworth's *Prelude*, Nicholson published in 1975 a (prose) autobiography covering his formative years up to his late teens[3], when he was sixty-one years of age. It was both retrospective and selective, but nonetheless hugely accomplished and entertaining. Yet, tantalisingly, the account ends before the author's literary career ever begins. There was to be no sequel from Nicholson, who was essentially a very private man, despite his gregariousness. His lifetime's collection of books and papers are preserved in academic literary archives, but he culled them ruthlessly beforehand and they represent only a fragment of their former volume and range; they reveal little about Nicholson's inner life, especially his personal life during the period before his marriage in 1956 at the age of forty-two.

Despite some accomplished verse drama during the 1940s and early 1950s, Nicholson regarded himself primarily as a poet, but relied upon freelance journalism and prose book authorship for his main income. As a teenager, he contracted serious and near-fatal tuberculosis which left him in very poor health thereafter, denying him the opportunity of a university education and a conventional job role such as in teaching or within an academic institution.

Intensive literary 'networking' was a striking and pervasive feature of the whole of Nicholson's life, in spite of his underprivileged background and his self-chosen remote location. A vibrant and close-knit nationwide web interlinked the leading writers and artists of the period. T.S. Eliot was at this web's centre, but other notable participants included E. Martin Browne, Kathleen Raine, Anne Ridler, Ben and Winifred Nicholson, Barbara Hepworth, Michael and Janet Roberts, Brother George Every (especially) and very many more. Nicholson became a prolific letter writer in order to maintain contact with all his scattered and distant friends, but sadly very little of this vast correspondence has survived systematic and deliberate destruction both by Nicholson and by his closest friend and correspondent, George Every.

In 1968/1969, a Cambridge English graduate, Philip Gardner, undertook a PhD at Liverpool University, entitled *The poetry and drama of Norman Nicholson, with reference to contemporary English provincial poetry and the Christian drama of the 1940s and 1950s*[4]. Gardner was allowed virtually unfettered access to the extensive papers then held by Nicholson himself and those of his lifelong friend and mentor, George Every, and of his friend from childhood and early literary champion, Mrs Bessie Schiff (Satterthwaite). The bulk of this correspondence having since been destroyed, Gardner's thesis remains one of the few surviving sources, and has therefore of necessity been referred to extensively in connection with this critical biography.

Gardner went on to publish in the United States in 1973 a book based on his Nicholson thesis which, for the following forty years, remained the only published full-length critical study of Nicholson and his work[5]. Gardner himself from 1964 followed an academic career at the Memorial University of Newfoundland, becoming an Associate Professor and later full Professor in their English Literature faculty and a world-respected commentator and academic authority on the work of E.M. Forster, as well as on Philip Larkin and Edmund Blunden. The dust cover of Gardner's published Nicholson book states that Dr Gardner was a personal friend of Norman Nicholson from as early as 1957.

Curiously though, the content of Gardner's book on Nicholson was significantly abridged compared with his thesis in order to cut out a significant episode in Nicholson's early manhood, this being his close relationship with a vivacious and talented school teacher, Enrica Garnier, which suddenly and unexpectedly ended just after the end of World War II. This information was not completely excised in that an end note to the 'Nicholson's Life' introductory section does mention a friendship 'of strong private importance' with Enrica Garnier[6], but the contrast here between the content of the thesis and that of the book is nonetheless striking.

Distinct parallels emerge between Nicholson's life and that of some of his contemporaries, particularly fellow regional poets such as Charles Causley, Jack Clemo, Basil Bunting, R.S. Thomas and even Hugh MacDiarmid. The similarities between Causley and Nicholson are particularly close: both had a working class background; both were autodidacts; both were inextricably attached to the towns of their birth, and even their poetic styles were very similar. The distinguished American poet and critic, Dana Gioia has acutely observed (in discussing Causley, but a parallel insight into Nicholson's work is obvious here too)[7]:

> *There is no better way to approach Causley's poetry than through his life, because few modern poets have been so meaningfully rooted in one time and place. Charles Stanley Causley was born in 1917 in the Cornish market town of Launceston where, except for six years of military service, he has lived ever since…*

Nicholson was most certainly one of the foremost of these 'few modern poets'.

And very few (if any) UK poets barely out of their twenties have been elected to Fellowships of the Royal Society of Literature - this honour was similarly bestowed on Causley, but not until he was around forty-one years of age. The young Nicholson's debut as a published poet led almost immediately to that substantial honour. Nicholson's early work positively exudes a vivid sense of place, deft originality of craftsmanship and overall accomplishment as in, for example:

Brown clouds are blown against the bright fells
Like Celtic psalms from drowned western isles.
The slow rain falls like memory
And floods the becks and flows to the sea,
And there on the coast of Cumberland mingle
The fresh and the salt, the cinders and the shingle.
(Extract, from Five Rivers, 1944)

Or:

...The long cord of the water, the shepherd's numerals
That run upstream, through the singing decades
of dialect
He [i.e., Wordsworth] knew, beneath mutation
of year and season,
Flood and drought, frost and fire and thunder,
The frothy blossom on the rowan and the
reddening of the berries,
The silt, the sand, the slagbanks and the shingle,
And the wild catastrophes of the breaking mountains,
There stands the base and root of the living rock,
Thirty thousand feet of solid Cumberland.
(Closing lines of *To the River Duddon*, 1944)

This remarkable early promise was not fully sustained in the later years, and this critical biography attempts to find a possible explanation. But, this is not an 'authorised' biography: all of Nicholson's literary works are protected by copyright, which his literary executor and agents have declined to lift for this writer. That has, in one sense, been an impediment, especially with regard to the evaluation of Nicholson's exquisite craftsmanship, but it has also brought with it a valuable opportunity to tell the full story without constraint.

An authorised biography was published in late 2013[8], when this one had reached final draft form. I offer no overall critique of Jones' biography, but have amended my draft to include instances where I have to take issue with some of the 'facts' stated therein.

I have attempted in this book to tread a tightrope between academic rigour and general interest; between reference reading for a purpose and leisure browsing; between factual dryness and reasonably-colourful readability. The first Chapter describes at some considerable (but I trust not tiresome) length the town of Millom and its history, which I feel is essential to set the scene and context of Nicholson's literary life.

So, hoping fervently that I have succeeded just a little in this task, for better or for worse, here it all is.

1

Nicholson's Local Habitation – Millom and Environs

Millom did not exist until about 1860. It grew from nothing but a few cottages to a small but thriving industrial town as a direct consequence of the rapidly developing technology of the First Industrial Revolution. Before c.1860 the place was an isolated coastal hamlet known as Holborn Hill, surrounded by useless marshland. The ancient edifice of Millom Castle and the adjacent Holy Trinity Church had stood there since medieval times. The Whitehaven and Furness Junction Railway had reached out its network to this remote area in 1850, probably in order to service the local tile and brick works.

The history of the town of Millom is in large part a microcosm of that of the whole of industrial and post-industrial Britain: this very industrialisation both depended upon, and was made possible by, the availability of cheap, bulk steel. Before Darby's (1709) invention of utilising coal to smelt iron, wood charcoal had to be used for this purpose. The very limited amounts of iron that emerged from the early stone-built 19th century charcoal blast furnaces[9] could only be converted into steel, which was a far stronger and more versatile industrial material than iron, by a slow, laborious and expensive refining process, typically via crucibles. All this changed when, in 1855, Henry Bessemer patented a completely new method for bulk steelmaking by means of blowing air through molten iron in a tilting converter rather like a concrete mixer. But at inception the Bessemer process required iron very low in phosphorus content. Millom happened to stand amidst underground deposits of millions of tons of high-grade, low-phosphorus iron ore (hematite) which could be smelted in blast furnaces into superior quality iron, which in turn could be converted via this new 'acid' Bessemer process into very high-quality bulk steel. Ore mines were quickly sunk all around Millom and they proliferated and prospered.

Two blast furnaces were erected at Millom and began hematite iron production in 1867. Originally, they were manually-charged open-topped masonry structures[10] lined with firebricks, with outputs of only around 150 tons a week each. Advances in iron making technology quickly made these furnaces obsolete and in 1874 they were replaced by four furnaces, each of far greater capacity, which used the formerly-wasted carbon monoxide gas emitted to pre-heat the air blast via giant stoves. In 1890, Millom Ironworks merged with nearby Askam Ironworks, along with all the associated hematite ore mines including Florence and Ullcoats mine, further north from Millom, at Egremont.

By 1890, Millom had six blast furnaces and Askam a further four. Combined production capacity was around 350,000 tons per annum. Nicholson, in *WEC* recalls that his paternal grandparents had first settled in the then-booming Millom in 1867, and according to his father, his own father (Nicholson's grandfather), then employed at Millom Ironworks, had once been offered the job of Works Manager of Askam Ironworks but had not thought his level of educational attainment sufficient, so had modestly declined.

At the end of the First World War it was decided to close down the Askam works and to concentrate production at the Millom site. The derelict Askam site was finally demolished in 1938, and all that remains of these operations today is 'Askam Pier', which in reality is where all the former waste slag was tipped into the sea.

In addition to the local ore mines, Millom Ironworks owned ore mines in Spain until 1951, namely, the Alquife Mines along with associated private railways and loading facilities at the port of Almeria.

The UK iron and steel industry was nationalised by the Labour Government in 1951 but it was returned to private ownership a few years later by a new Conservative Government. Millom was included in that first nationalisation, and, after return to the private sector, became the Millom Hematite Ore and Iron Company Limited, which was acquired by an engineering company, the Cranleigh Group, in 1959.

But Millom's staple industry by then was in long-term economic decline. Not long after the worldwide adoption of the Bessemer process, further developments in steelmaking production technology, along with cheaper foreign imports, had slowly but inexorably been shrinking Millom's traditional market for low phosphorus hematite iron.

Acid open hearth furnaces then supplanted the Bessemer process and were at first a boon to Millom, as they initially demanded low-phosphorus iron. But, as with the Bessemer process, widespread use of differently constituted process vessel linings enabled steel making plants to use far cheaper, relatively impure, iron. Later bulk steelmaking processes, too, could readily use cheaper high-phosphorus iron, together with another significant advantage in that they could be charged with far higher proportions of relatively far cheaper scrap ferrous metal.

World War Two only temporarily arrested this process of long-term decline. The Millom Ironworks management foresaw the very serious implications and were progressive and innovative in their response: they fully exploited their product strengths, building an iron foundry to cast ingot moulds and bottom plates, which still needed to be cast from low-phosphorus, hematite iron, their superior longevity in use offsetting their higher cost. At Millom they also made specialist grades of refined iron in Tropenas converters, and even generated electricity from all their blast furnace gas, selling the surplus on to the National Grid. As late as the early 1960s, they installed a completely new, then-state-of-the-art blast furnace, capable of efficiently producing up to 7,000 tons of pig iron each week.

Furthermore, the Millom Ironworks management had the vision and the nerve to contemplate the probability of total plant closure, unless drastic changes could be made, and saw their salvation as being in a newly invented still experimental steelmaking process, called Spray Steelmaking, in which molten iron running from the blast furnace was sprayed through special nozzles so as to be decarburised by injected oxygen and turned into steel. This process had been conceived and experimentally proven by the British Iron and Steel Research Association, and a pilot plant had subsequently been installed alongside the Millom blast furnaces. Longer term plans even included a revolutionary continuous casting machine, to which the molten steel, instead of being cast into ingots, could be directly transferred for immediate and continuous further processing into semi-finished solidified sections. Far ahead of its time, this concept was much later to be successfully deployed in niche-market 'mini-mills' involving electric-arc steelmaking furnaces feeding directly adjacent continuous casting machines.

Sadly, politics and (probably) vested and powerful interests within the U.K. steel industry intervened. The Iron and Steel Board, composed mainly of representatives of the major steelmaking cartels, for an exceedingly long period stalled and refused to support the spray steelmaking project, refusing also to recommend vital Government grant aid. Millom Ironworks had not been designated for re-nationalisation and consequent absorption into the newly-formed (1967) British Steel Corporation, so it remained in private ownership and therefore was obliged to fend for itself financially. As a result of the market pressures already outlined, the works was losing its owners substantial and ultimately unacceptable amounts of money. The Government's indifference to these innovative development plans proved to be the last straw, and total closure of the works took place in 1968 /69. Even the spray steelmaking pilot plant was abandoned, and the process was never successfully adopted elsewhere.[11]

This extract from the *Hansard* record of a House of Lords Second Reading debate of the Bill for the forthcoming steel industry nationalisation (Lord Royle, addressing the House[12]) most lucidly and vividly illustrates Millom's desperate situation:

> *May I, as briefly as possible, tell a story which is critical of the larger companies and of the existing Iron and Steel Board. I hope to show how the "big boys" behave towards their little brothers. During the past few years the British Iron and Steel Research Association have experimented with a completely new and revolutionary system of steel production - for brevity I will call it the spray system. It is fairly well known now. I have not the time to describe it, even if I had the technical knowledge. For the purposes of my argument it is sufficient to say that when the process was perfected all the companies connected with B.I.S.R.A. - they were the large ones; almost all*

of them had the opportunity to try it out. They were not interested; they showed no interest. In spite of its great advance in economic saving in steel production, they still seemed to be committed completely to existing methods.

This process puts in the shade the great Austrian L.D. process which has done so much to establish the economy of that country and other countries. I wonder whether a nationalised steel industry would have failed to show interest! The lack of interest by the large companies is as great an argument for this Bill as any that could be produced. But at Millom there was a much smaller company producing pig iron from indigenous ore. It employed about 1,000 men from the small town of Millom, with a population of 9,000 or 10,000. This town is isolated from any other industrial area by sea, lakes and mountains, and is wholly dependent on this plant. The firm had struck a difficult time, due to the importation of pig iron from Scandinavia, Eastern Europe and from South Africa.

In passing, may I say that in my view there is a close relationship in politics here, because my information is that Southern Rhodesia is exporting pig iron to South Africa and South Africa is sending her pig iron to Britain. Cheaper labour in ore mining and pig iron production in the countries I have mentioned brings about a cheaper price. In my view, this comes near to dumping. Two out of three blast furnaces were shut down in Millom and unemployment and redundancy resulted. It appeared almost as though the town was dying - a modern Jarrow. A brilliant, youngish managing director[13]*, with experience in South Wales and in India, saw the B.I.S.R.A. process, and at the expense of his own firm he installed a pilot plant. It is a resounding and unqualified success. This is admitted by everybody who knows anything about steel production. The national and scientific Press have been enthusiastic. Articles have appeared in The Times, the Daily Telegraph, the Financial Times, the Guardian, the Observer, the New Scientist, the Statist, and note, my Lords, the Steel Times, the industry's own paper. Millom applied to the Iron and Steel Board to expand to a full plant - a works to expand, a town to be saved. The Board deferred the decision in a way which amounts to a refusal - in these days, when the cry for technological advance is so clear, it was the Board who turned it down. It was not the Minister, in spite of what the noble Lord, Lord Erroll of Hale, said. As I tried to say in an intervention, Millom have appealed to the Minister against that decision and are waiting for a reply. So it is obvious who turned them down, and I say this without any fear of contradiction: it was the existing Iron and Steel Board who turned down their application for expansion. It would appear that they were passing the buck to the Minister, who will have the powers under the new Bill.*

At this late stage of the activity some of the larger companies are now having a look at the new process,

I believe in an endeavour to cut out Millom from extension, they being new in the steel production field.' The Times' newspaper said: "This is the most exciting new development in world iron and steel production for many years. It is being held back from commercial development by the Iron and Steel Board. World-wide interest has been aroused." The kiss of life to the steel industry could be slow, lingering death to Millom if they are not allowed to proceed. I want to say as strongly as I can that justice demands that the initiative they took should be rewarded. Millom is scheduled for industrial development under the 1966 Act. There is therefore some responsibility lying with the Board of Trade. I cannot believe that my right honourable friend, Mr Douglas Jay, will let Millom die. It would cost a million pounds to set up expansion, with £400,000 working capital, much of which the company can raise. It would cost much more in redundancy and unemployment payments, and the removal of a thousand families, plus the loss to retail traders in the town, and all the resultant misery.

This is such a technological advance that the Minister of Technology must be interested, and since Millom are the pioneers they must have priority in that interest and help. But the main burden falls upon my right honourable friend the Minister of Power. He can overrule the Iron and Steel Board. Using this Second Reading debate on this new Bill, my appeal is that this small, independent company may have its chance, preferably now, and certainly under

> *the new Bill with its new concept. A works, a town can be saved; and at the same time a revolutionary process can be expanded for the wellbeing of the industry and the nation as a whole. It is important to notice in our arguments for nationalisation that this has happened under the old regime. It is a strange commentary that the new regime, nationalisation, could save Millom and others like it from the old so-called independent regime. Ye Gods! They talk about competition! It looks as if they are terrified of it.*

All these detailed economic and political facts relating to Millom's industrial history of course cannot really begin adequately to describe the catastrophic effects of closure upon the lives of almost every one of the town's inhabitants. The ore mines and the ironworks were the very reason for the town and the community coming into being and they had formed its lifeblood for the past century. Their closure left Millom with little or no means of continued existence, save as somewhere for a few thousand households to live and either to eke out their poverty-level State benefits or for their few marketable breadwinners to travel to sundry distant locations in search of employment.[14]

Many UK communities which were formerly reliant on heavy industry have since suffered this brutal fate - the coal mining towns and villages of South Wales, County Durham and South Yorkshire, for example. Similarly affected, too, but closer to Millom, were Cumbrian coal and iron ore mining towns such as Cleator Moor, Frizington, and many others.

Nicholson's own father was a shopkeeper, but was, albeit indirectly, very much reliant upon Millom's predominant industry. Nicholson himself had witnessed the human suffering caused by the Depression of the 1930s, and he feared a return to similar dire circumstances when the Ironworks was closed-down. Some of his finest poems are for him uncharacteristic ones - indignant, almost bitter, lamentations which contrast markedly with his usual themes, being poems of heartfelt personal protest about the arbitrary and cataclysmic closure of a traditional and staple industry. In similar vein he once warned of the potentially-deadly environmental effects (as he perceived them) of the sinister new industry in the form of the atomic facility at nearby Sellafield.[15]

But Nicholson was inevitably removed from directly experiencing the hard labours of workaday Millom, as had his father. Nicholson recounts in *WEC* that his father resisted and was excused conscription in World War One, but as an alternative was ordered to work part time at the Ironworks: an arduous manual occupation for which he was exceedingly unsuitable, both physically and temperamentally.

Nonetheless, many of Nicholson immediate family were directly employed in Millom's core industries. One of his uncles had been an underground ore miner, and was killed as a result of a rock fall, in 1896. Another uncle was always described by Nicholson himself[16] as a skilled blacksmith at the Ironworks, but in the 1911 Census he was listed as a 'Blacksmith's Striker' which is not in fact a skilled blacksmith, but, rather, a kind of blacksmith's labourer.

Nicholson's paternal grandfather has already been mentioned in connection with his role at the Ironworks, and Nicholson wrote of his grandfather's close involvement with the works' horse powered haulage. Horses would, at that time, have been used extensively as cheaper and more flexible alternatives to steam locomotives, for example to move around and couple together individual railway wagons[17].

Nicholson also referred to his grandfather having been instrumental in organising the transportation of the very considerable amounts of rock and gravel needed to connect the Ironworks with the newly-developing Millom town centre, being built around the town's railway station about a mile inland. Later, Grandfather Nicholson became a blast furnace foreman, which was a demanding job of considerable responsibility.

In view of Nicholson's lack of direct experience of working life within the Ironworks, he can perhaps be excused a few howlers in his poetic depictions of it. For one example, in his Wordsworthian protest poem *'On the Dismantling of Millom Ironworks'* he mourns the passing of one hundred years of the Bessemer process, in spite of the fact that Millom Ironworks never manufactured any bulk steel, either by the Bessemer process, or by any other process, save latterly a very small amount, within that ill-fated experimental spray steelmaking pilot plant[18].

Millom Ironworks was in reality a specialist manufacturer of merchant pig iron, along with being an iron foundry; it was never a 'steelworks'.

In the same poem, Nicholson describes molten iron being at a temperature of one thousand degrees Fahrenheit, whereas in reality the melting point of iron is very much higher, at about 1500 degrees on the Celsius Scale, which equates to over 2700 degrees in Fahrenheit. Even for anyone experiencing molten ferrous metal from a fair distance - say, of a bus-length or two away - the intensity of both the heat and the infrared radiation from this molten metal feels colossal to the human body.

Current health and safety laws dictate that blast furnace workers must be swathed in all manner of special protective clothing, but, in the Millom Ironworks era, wooden-soled clogs were virtually the only commonly used personal protective equipment for blast furnace workpeople - rubber soles would immediately have melted and even leather ones would char and burn.

As Nicholson graphically describes in this poem, once a blast furnace is tapped, which typically happened at regular intervals all around the clock[19], the molten iron pours in pale orange torrents down the trenches which the blast furnace labourers have constructed for the purpose, using fresh dried sand, dug into the casting floor. The casting floor of the cast house is so named because once the iron was actually cast therein in 'pig beds' - primitive moulds made in the sand deriving from the image of a sow feeding all her little piglets, hence the term 'pig iron'.[20]

The closure of the Ironworks threw up to 650 people directly out of work, along with a further 300 at the Florence/Ullcoats Iron Ore Mine which subsequently was taken over by the nationalized British Steel Corporation. Closure inevitably tore the very heart out of the one-industry small town of Millom which was already reeling from the cessation of local iron ore mining.

The effects upon the plant's workers must have been profound and catastrophic, both economically and psychologically. Blast furnaces were operated by very close-knit 'crews' on a round-the-clock shift rota system aligned to a regular and hard routine of preparing for and accomplishing the already-described 'tapping' of molten slag and iron from the furnace, and clearing all the detritus away, re-instating everything in readiness for the next cast, interspersed by much-needed rest breaks between casts. Many hot, arduous and dangerous maintenance and repair jobs to the furnace cooling and the hot blast system also fell to the furnace crew. Traditional hierarchies of job roles and remuneration usually prevailed - the most senior crew member was the Furnace Keeper, who had overall charge of a particular furnace's manual workers and was responsible to the Plant Foreman for the safe and efficient conduct of that furnace's operations. If molten iron or slag came into contact with any trace of moisture the consequences were always explosive and often, in those days of minimal worker protection, gravely damaging to human skin and flesh. Blast furnaces were extremely temperamental and unpredictable for their operators fully to control (one reason why blast furnace Keepers were traditionally very handsomely paid) and the progress and properties of their molten contents had to be constantly and carefully monitored virtually at all costs, otherwise very severe problems could quickly and unexpectedly arise.

Workers started at the bottom of the furnace 'promotion line' as labourers and worked their way up by means of pure seniority/length of service into the more responsible and better-paid jobs. Particularly for the younger and fitter junior labourers, the work was tough, filthy, noisy, hot and hazardous. Moreover, it was totally 'occupationally-specific' in that no other industry would or could ever contemplate employing an expert Blast Furnace Keeper with twenty or thirty years' experience, except at a very small fraction of his former wages.[21] The Ironworks closure thus had obvious implications for all kinds of immense human suffering to the unfortunate former blast furnacemen, all of their dependants, and, ultimately, for the whole town.

It was largely elemental work - with fire, water and earth and this author's perception[22] is that it tended to shape the characters of those who undertook it - and lots of blast furnace workers were more than a little alarming to encounter at first meeting, but few were anything but totally transparent, moral, straightforward and, above-all, kind, caring and sociable individuals. Judging by all the Irish surnames which populated lists of blast furnace workers, many fanilies had originally been immigrants from that country.

From a macroeconomic perspective, all these events stem from unstoppable global economic and technological changes. Even if Millom Ironworks had been made part of the British Steel Corporation, the plant would doubtless have been closed down sooner or later along with most other UK iron and steel works, just as inevitably as cheap imported iron ore and changing production technologies had closed down the Hodbarrow hematite ore mines. Indirectly, Nicholson and his father and stepmother and their small business owed a big part, if not all, of their livelihoods to the money pumped into the Millom economy by the Ironworks. It has already been noted, above, that the closure of both the Ironworks and the hematite mines removed almost every reason for Millom's continued economic existence, yet, as Nicholson often emphasised, it remained an established community of people, with a right to a civilised life, and it would have been unthinkable simply to obliterate it from the map.

In 2014 virtually all that remains of Millom Ironworks is a tract of cleared ground: it is now a Nature Reserve. One poignant reminder has escaped the scrap merchants' clutches, though. This is a giant lump of iron[23], which must have been the very last contents of the biggest furnace, just before it was shut down. It must have been so massive as to defy any safe methods of salvage, and was therefore left where it was.

Nicholson was never really a fully accepted member of the working community of either the mines or of the ironworks, but both these Millom communities without a doubt spilled over into the overall social composition of the town, within which Nicholson did very much mingle and interact. For one most important instance, various non-conformist chapels had been established by the immigrant West Country mineworkers, and these were as much social organisations, as they were places of worship, just as the mines and the ironworks themselves were social settings as well as workplaces.

The sad plight of post-industrial Millom was commented upon by Nicholson in his BBC Radio 3 broadcasts *Letters from Cumberland*, which later appeared in print, in *The Listener.*[24] Here, Nicholson recounts events in his own life and in the town of Millom during the early 1970s, the town attempting to recover as best it could from all the severe body-blows of industrial decline. One major topic of these broadcasts relates to Millom's innovative but now largely forgotten hovercraft factory[25], which failed through probably being ahead of its time and through lack of finance, Nicholson refers too to that BBC Television *Look, Stranger*[26] documentary programme about himself as well as to the ambitious, but never fully-realised, plans for the town's economic regeneration, utilising for new industries the sites of the former Ironworks and ore mines.

Today, Millom remains a depressed area. Her Majesty's Prison at the site of a former wartime airfield by the nearby coastal village of Haverigg and some isolated pockets of leisure and tourism form the only significant sources of employment. Long ago, a leather tannery at Haverigg was established and it became a major employer. Later, mainly during the 1960s, there were a few large light industrial factories, such as Elbeo (c. 250 employees) and K Shoes (c. 500 employed) at nearby Askam, but, in 2013, even these are long-gone, with little significant large employers ever likely to replace them.

Twenty-five years after Nicholson's death, his only home during his lifetime, the little terraced house that is 14 St. George's Terrace is now (2013) a health food shop, with a small cafe in the ground floor back room, which retains the original coal fire into which Nicholson himself had stared all his life and the 'back-kitchen' once ruled over by his grandmother.

It has to be observed that Nicholson's high esteem for his fellow Millom inhabitants was not universally reciprocated by them, either during Nicholson's lifetime, or afterwards. A modest blue plaque commemorates his former house and his father's shop, and the town's small Folk Museum maintains a collection of Nicholson memorabilia, but otherwise the town seems to be less than enthusiastic in celebrating and publicising the life and work of one of its most distinguished inhabitants. One very notable exception is that a group of Nicholson's admirers and former friends and family formed a Norman Nicholson Society in 2006. The Society maintains a comprehensive website, and publishes an adroitly-edited and informative Journal, named *Comet*.

2

Nicholson's Formative Years, 1914-1932

A detailed and entertaining account of his early life was given by Nicholson himself in his autobiography, *WEC*. It is not proposed, either here or elsewhere in this study, to précis or to repeat the contents of that book, save to recount some notable features, and to introduce a few new ones.

WEC was not published until 1975, when Nicholson was sixty-one years of age. The reviewer of the book in the *Times Literary Supplement*[27] praised it fulsomely:

> *(It) deserves to become a minor classic...*

But in spite of such accolades the book was not a commercial success, selling only about three thousand copies; it all too soon fell out of print until it was reissued by Faber and Faber thirty-three years later, in 2008.

Nicholson himself considered that *WEC* richly deserved a reprint, as evidenced by a letter to fellow poet Matt Simpson dated 29 November, 1983, preserved in the Manchester University John Rylands Library.[28] This includes a rueful comment that interest of the general populace in his work seemed to dwindle to zero, anywhere south of about Manchester.

WEC invites comparison with Laurie Lee's *Cider with Rosie*, published in 1959; however, Nicholson's spare and lucid prose style contrasts markedly with Laurie Lee's graphic but rather florid one[29]. Nicholson's experiences of growing-up only ever in passing and never in any great detail describe his own, personal, inner life and all its associated passions, urges and feelings. This reticence to express in his writings his own inner feelings is (as mentioned many times in this book) typical of much of Nicholson's *oeuvre*. *WEC* rather abruptly screams to a halt in the autumn of 1932 with the eighteen-year-old Nicholson's return to his native Millom after his lengthy hospitalisation in a faraway private TB Sanatorium, at Linford, in Hampshire's New Forest.

An author's note at the beginning of *WEC* informs that 'some of the Christian names have been changed.' Nicholson in fact had disguised the real name of a young female sanatorium patient, described in *WEC* as 'Celia'[30]. This was Sylvia Lubelsky[31]. In *WEC*, Nicholson describes her as an intelligent and very handsome woman of around twenty, with whom he immediately felt immensely comfortable. Nicholson goes on in *WEC* to assert that Sylvia's extra few years of age, as well as her tactful nature, had prevented his falling in love with her.

Fortunately, at least for biographers, Sylvia Lubelsky assiduously kept the many letters she had received from Nicholson, both whilst at Linford and afterwards, when they had remained in fairly close, if irregular, touch, although strictly as friends, their lives since Linford having taken very divergent paths.

Nicholson in *WEC,* fondly describes as revelatory these idyllic days spent in his new friend Sylvia's company. This coincided with his awaiting his forthcoming return to Millom. He credits Sylvia, too, with having inspired in him a lifelong, deep, affection for all that classical music had to offer.

Sylvia's letters reveal a somewhat different picture to that painted selectively by Nicholson in *WEC.* The contemporaneous, unexpurgated, feelings of Nicholson, the lusty eighteen-year-old, are plainly always apparent within these letters; thus, they differ markedly from Nicholson's version of events, as recounted in his autobiography: a version written from the perspective of Nicholson as a sixty-one-year-old married man.

The correspondence between Sylvia and the teenage Nicholson begins with internal notes between them of gushing intimacy - on Nicholson's part, at least - on Linford Sanatorium notepaper. He addresses Sylvia in tones of considerable affection in many of these early notes.

Nicholson's denial in *WEC* of his ever actually 'falling in love' with 'Celia' seems less than credible, after even cursory examination of the content of these significant letters. It is clear that Sylvia did not want that kind of relationship and that she feared that her new friend was seriously falling in love with her. Subsequent letters indicate that Sylvia once made it very clear that their relationship could not continue on a romantic basis. Norman pleaded for its continuance on the basis of pure friendship, but the still-impassioned tone of this - and subsequent- correspondence indicates plainly the intensity of his true feelings for Sylvia.

Sylvia eventually was discharged from Linford; she subsequently married and had children. Norman, by the late 1930s, had embarked upon a serious relationship with another young woman, a pretty and gifted school teacher, namely, Enrica Garnier.

But Nicholson and Sylvia kept amicably in touch, albeit intermittently, for the following fifty years or so. Their correspondence immediately following Nicholson's return to Millom from Linford was both copious and frequent. Nicholson obviously found great delight and solace in it. At that time Nicholson must have been feeling bereft to be back in Millom and missing Sylvia's company grievously. On more than one occasion he gently chides Sylvia for her tardiness in responding to his very long and largely illegible letters. Although suffused with deep affection and warmth, Nicholson's's letters to Sylvia do seem to be strangely impersonal in tone and content, as if deliberately steering clear of any matters of their mutual interpersonal feelings.

Music, nature and literature therefore tended to be the main, rather neutral, topics of their correspondence;

Nicholson for example frequently included snippets of musical notation in his letters, relating to works he had encountered on the radio. An act of very great generosity, given the high price then of a good quality gramophone and the particular circumstances of the relationship, was that Sylvia's then-boyfriend Maurice Elvey,[32] (later, her husband) very generously presented Nicholson with a fine new gramophone as a personal gift.

Many decades passed, until in 1978 Nicholson delivered a reading of his poetry in St. John's, Smith Square, in London's Westminster, which was attended by Sylvia, along with her immediate family.

In *WEC*, Nicholson made mention too of his rich 'Uncle Dick'. This was in fact his stepmother's uncle, Richard Sobey, a West Country (Devon) tin miner who had been one of four brothers who, like many West Country hard rock miners, had settled in Millom to work in the then booming iron ore mines, in 1869. Richard subsequently had violently quarrelled with the mine manager and as a result he left Hodbarrow to seek mine work overseas, in Mexico, where in and around the city of Pachuca an expatriate community of Devonian and Cornish settlers had grown up in order to work the local silver mines. His son Richard Thomas remained at school in Millom, but upon leaving school he was denied a job at the Hodbarrow mines simply because he was a Sobey and because the man in charge still harboured so much ill will towards that particular family. So Richard emigrated to join his father in Mexico. After years of very hard work and thrift, the family's life savings were invested in ownership of one of the mines. The Sobey mine fortuitously struck silver almost immediately, making Uncle Dick and his family a substantial fortune, enabling them to sell-up and return permanently to live very comfortably indeed in England.

To this day, Cornish pasties (albeit with uniquely-Mexican fillings) remain an incongruous but integral part of the traditional gastronomy of Pachuca, and the transplanted Methodist churches and associated graveyards bear poignant witness to the privations endured by these Cornish and other West Country settlers.[33] Passenger lists from *RMS Olympic*, White Star Line's sister ship to the notorious *Titanic*, indicate that Richard T. Sobey and his wife Catherine, both aged forty-two, had sailed *en route* for Mexico City as second class (i.e. fairly high-class) passengers from Southampton in 1912.[34] This must have been their return journey from a home visit, prior to the family selling up in Mexico and returning home. The Sobeys nearby Bournemouth home location was ultimately to help determine the choice of Linford as the young Nicholson's TB Sanatorium.

Linford Sanatorium was, in its time, a select and highly regarded private TB Sanatorium run by a Dr Arthur De Winton Snowden CBE (1872-1950) who was referred to by Nicholson enigmatically in *WEC* as 'Dr S'. Dr Snowden was for many years a leading member of the British Medical Association and a senior officer of its Tuberculosis Section.

From 1899, Linford had been one of the pioneers in the UK of the *Nordrach* method of treatment for TB and was initially owned and operated by Dr Mander Smyth, who had himself been both a patient and later a Medical Officer at Dr Otto Walther's sanatorium at Nordrach in Germany's Black Forest. Dr Snowden underwent exactly the same experiences when his own TB flared up again shortly after he qualified as a doctor, in 1902. The *Nordrach* treatment method was not termed as such by Nicholson in *WEC* but was fully described by him. Although complete rest and maximising exposure to natural winds and fresh air was a key feature of this treatment regime, it was by no means the only one. Great emphasis was also placed on building up the general health and constitution of the patient by means of regular, substantial and nutritious meals and lots of full cream milk to drink. Progress towards this was monitored by regular checks on weight gain or loss. The aim was to bring down body temperature to normal levels from the typical febrile ones which TB caused, and temperatures therefore were constantly monitored. Those who responded favourably to this treatment were allowed carefully controlled spells of walking and other exercise. Complete rest and isolation from the cares and worries of 'normal' non-institutional life was encouraged, and this probably added greatly to the overall therapeutic effects.

But the stark fact was that, before the discovery and widespread use of antibiotics from the mid - 1940s onwards, TB or 'consumption' was a killer disease, with a plethora of treatment options, especially for those able to pay for them privately, but with no known cure, and the young Nicholson (as he later discovered) was not expected to survive for too many years following diagnosis. The fact that, against all the odds, he did survive clearly shaped Nicholson's entire future outlook on life and helped determine his eventual spiritual and artistic direction.

However, the debilitating physical legacy of the TB was to remain with Nicholson for the rest of his life, in the form of chronic wheezing and shortness of breath, very limited stamina and constant vulnerability to colds and flu catching hold in his damaged lungs with severe consequences,

Curiously, (in fact, rather astonishingly), Nicholson's entry in the current *Dictionary of National Biography*[35] alleges that as a result of his tuberculosis one of his lungs had been removed. Though the author of the account may have conceivably had access to hitherto private information that this actually happened there exists no other evidence to indicate that this actually ever did occur.[36] It seems unlikely that Nicholson ever could, or would, have kept such a serious event a secret. Unless further explanation or evidence emerges, one might reasonably infer that the author of this piece was either mistaken or had been misinformed.

Nicholson discovered much later in life that the cost of funding his extended private treatment in Linford had nearly exhausted his father's life savings[37], but that fact had never been disclosed to him at the time.

As recently as 2010, Linford still operated as a care and nursing home for the elderly. It has since been converted into residential flats.

To the young Nicholson, Linford in c. 1930 had acted both as a substitute for university and as a kind of finishing school, teaching him to mix confidently within all kinds of social circles, including those far more elevated than his own back in working-class Millom. Although in a way successfully treated for the actual tuberculosis, as noted already, Nicholson's overall health was indeed totally devastated by this condition. He had been instructed upon his return to Millom closely to maintain his Linford regime, especially to continue to take considerable rest and to strive only to breathe clean, fresh air. Disabled people like Nicholson received little or no state financial support in pre-Welfare-State England, so Norman had to rely totally upon the financial resources of his parents.

Thus the events of Nicholson's early life very clearly helped shape his entire personality as an adult, and consequently his eventual literary output. Some further profound influences were very probably (and as touched-upon in this book's Introduction) the loss during his infancy of his natural mother and his subsequent upbringing as an only-child by his no-nonsense, outwardly-fierce, grandmother; his buttoned-up, rather-odd father and his somewhat-detached stepmother. To any sensitive and highly intelligent child, almost irrespective of the particular psychological theories one cares to use, this was arguably a powerful recipe for the formation of significant psychological idiosyncrasies. Furthermore, his contracting TB as a young teenager, and subsequent isolation in a sanatorium, can be seen as retarding to some degree his development into a fully-mature and balanced adult. An old psychological chestnut - the 'nature v nurture' controversy - emerges in this regard: emotional deprivation from infancy onwards may well have led to the young Nicholson attaching himself to almost anyone at all who showed him kindness or affection,[38] and to his resorting to self-nurturing by withdrawing into a closely-guarded private world of his own making - albeit a very well-formed world that was a construct of his considerable imagination and high intellect.

A speculative neurobiological perspective is possible too: seeing Nicholson as falling within the autistic spectrum, perhaps indicating Asperger's Syndrome, which often is characterised by high intellect, narrow range of interests, particular expertise in something (language/poetry/public recitation in his case) and some vulnerabilities during social interaction. Nicholson was certainly viewed as something of a loner, at least socially, within his home town. Asperger's does tend to run in families, and it is possible that both Nicholson's grandmother and her son, Nicholson's father, may in their very different ways have exhibited it and have passed that characteristic on to Norman.

3

The Cast: In Rough Order of Appearance

This - necessarily - long chapter seeks to detail the adult Nicholson's significant influencers, in roughly chronological order in his life. Apart from expanding the biographical details of these key 'movers and shapers' it may help to evaluate their respective impacts upon both Nicholson's work, and his own self. The Chapter has been split into sub-chapters, each devoted to the person concerned. Many of these Nicholson-influencers of course often did so in conjunction with others, and inevitably there will be overlaps with the content of other chapters and some unavoidable instances of repetition, but it is hoped this approach may nonetheless serve usefully to outline who was who in Nicholson's extraordinary life.

3.01 Bessie Satterthwaite

Bessie Satterthwaite was a Millom contemporary of Nicholson, and a loyal friend who stalwartly championed his poetry from its outset. Her initiative in introducing Nicholson to George Every determined the entire course of Nicholson's future literary life and career.

Clara B. Satterthwaite was born in 1915 in Millom. Bessie, as she invariably was known, was a year younger than Nicholson, and followed the route Nicholson himself but for illness might well have taken, from Millom to university and thence into a teaching career. In 1933 she went up to Manchester University to read English. However, her father died in 1936, and she was forced by financial circumstances to take up a paid teaching post, which she did in Whitehaven, about 45 minutes by train from Millom. Bessie still regularly visited Millom at weekends. Gardner's thesis mentions this information, and that Bessie participated in Workers' Educational Association activities in Whitehaven; she may, therefore, have been instrumental, during the 1940s in arranging for Nicholson to be hired by the WEA to lecture at their classes in the St Bees and Whitehaven areas[39].

Bessie and Norman were constant companions during the 1930s. She was of strong religious faith and doubtless Nicholson's gradual reaffirmation of his own belief during the years leading up to 1940 drew them together. For example, Gardner's thesis quotes some otherwise unpublished lines, both personally affectionate and fervently religious which Nicholson wrote for

Bessie as Christmas greetings to accompany a picture of Raphael's 'Crucifixion'.

Bessie once described[40] the young Nicholson as markedly different in almost all respects, to other Millom boys and by far the cleverest boy in his class, mentioning too that these traits did not necessarily endear him to his peers.

Bessie and Nicholson eventually went their separate ways in life: Nicholson became attached to another teacher and English Literature enthusiast, Enrica Garnier, whilst Bessie, in the summer of 1944 married a clergyman, Leonard Maro Schiff in West Durham. The Revd. (later, Canon) Schiff was then parish priest of the mining village of Spennymoor. He and Bessie had first met via the Student Christian Movement.

Leonard Schiff's eventful and accomplished career led him to work in influential ecclesiastical positions in India, and for a time Bessie herself was Headmistress of Bishop Cotton School for Girls in Bangalore, Southern India. They returned to live in the UK, c.1960, and Leonard eventually became Principal of the College of the Ascension in Selly Oak, Birmingham, as well as Chaplain to Birmingham's Aston University.

Bessie's brother, John Richard (b.1925) became Bishop of Gibraltar in Europe, and at the same time, automatically Bishop of Fulham. Nicholson himself in 1948 became godfather to Bessie and Leonard's daughter, Anna, indicating that Bessie had remained a close Nicholson family friend.

Leonard and Bessie moved to Millom and later Ulverston, following Leonard's retirement, where both were involved in voluntary community work. Bessie became a (Labour) Millom Town Councillor. In 1997, the Schiffs moved to Exeter, where Leonard Schiff died in July 2002, aged ninety-three. Bessie herself died in 2010, shortly before her ninety-fifth birthday.

Bessie and Nicholson and their respective families remained in regular touch until Nicholson's death in 1987. A stray / surviving letter to George Every from Nicholson dated 1963[41] mentions that Bessie had recently called upon the Nicholson household – and that Bessie's mother had died recently, after a distressing illness, and that 'John' (possibly her brother, Bishop John) had said a Requiem for her in 'The Old Church' (presumably Holy Trinity, Millom).

In 1977, the local newspaper[42] reported some disparaging and dismissive comments made by one particular Millom Town Councillor concerning the recent decision of that Council rather reluctantly to 'honour' Nicholson by placing a bronze head of him made and donated to them by the sculptress Joan Palmer on permanent display in the Town Library. An indignant rebuke from Bessie followed in *Letters to the Editor,* in which she soundly rebutted these rather crass and prejudiced (but, it seems, not uncommon) attitudes towards Millom's most distinguished son.

As well as assiduously championing Nicholson's talents, Bessie was a patient, helpful and hospitable adviser over many years to many assorted academic researchers into Nicholson's life and works[43].

3.02 Brother George Every, S.S.M

George Every's very close friendship with Nicholson lasted for almost fifty years, until Nicholson's death in 1987. Every (1909-2003) was a somewhat shadowy and reclusive character, which somewhat inhibits effective biographical commentary. But he was undoubtedly an immense influence upon Nicholson's entire intellectual and literary life. His influence, too, upon the whole British literary and religious scene over a period of well over thirty years until the 1970s, was both deep-seated and pervasive, yet to date it has received little scholarly attention.

It has already been recounted that Nicholson first came to Every's attention in 1937. George Every was by then an Anglo-Catholic monk at the Monastery of the Society of the Sacred Mission (S.S.M.) at Kelham Hall in Nottinghamshire, where he was a tutor (the S.S.M. operated a theological college for training both home and overseas Anglican clergy) and he was what would now be termed their 'outreach co-ordinator' as well as a teacher and lecturer there. He also was an author of some standing, on history, theology and literature, and a regular lecturer at the Student Christian Movement's annual conferences at Swanwick in Derbyshire, especially during the 1930s.

Every had arrived at Kelham as a novice in 1929, after taking a degree at University College, Exeter, where he was taught by Christopher Dawson, the distinguished cultural historian and educational theorist. He became a full member of the Society as a lay brother in 1933. Kelham had been founded c. 1894 by Fr. Herbert Kelly

(1860-1950), whom the young George Every had first met there as a student.

The controversial former Bishop of Edinburgh, Richard Holloway, is just one of Kelham's numerous and distinguished worldwide alumni. Another is the Rev. Canon Professor Vincent Noel Harold Strudwick (b. 1932), who returned after his ordination to Kelham where he was a Tutor (1959-1963) and Sub-Warden (1963-1970). Strudwick became a close friend and colleague of George Every and, upon Every's death in 2003, wrote in *The Church Times* a warm, witty and well-informed tribute to George's long life:

> *With his eccentric manner and a pronounced stammer, George seemed to live more in the preoccupations and concerns of the sixth than the twentieth century. Many of his students over the years, however, began to understand something of his approach to history and culture, and the way the purposes of God are teased out in all of this; they also discovered that he could be an affectionate and loyal friend.*

> *Eliot (like Charles Williams, C. S. Lewis, and John Heath Stubbs) was a friend, and encouraged him to persevere with writing poetry, and not to worry about recognition. "If you are a good poet, you are good enough to be neglected," Eliot wrote.*
> *It was a source of great joy to his Anglican friends that the community at Oscott welcomed him with such generosity*

and valued both his scholarship and holiness. They, too, began to build up a collection of "George stories". (My own include searching Nottingham pubs for his false teeth, which he had inadvertently left behind after lunch during a conference.) Yet curiously, unlike most of us, he seemed to get less eccentric as he got older.

At his funeral mass at Oscott, the Bishop of Northampton (and former Rector of the Seminary) preached a sermon to a large congregation of friends and former students from both his homes. Some of us met at lunch, putting faces to names we had known for years through George's conversation. It was often not clear whether they belonged to the twentieth century or the sixth; but those we missed we may perhaps hope to meet, with George, later.

Every earlier in his life was a contributor to The Criterion magazine; his late-1930s draft play about Nicholas Ferrar's Little Gidding community and the fugitive King Charles' encounter with it, *Stalemate*, probably helped evoke T.S. Eliot's interest in that place which resulted in Eliot's eponymous Four Quartets poem. But Every is rarely given even partial credit by academics for this inspirational input.

In 1939, Eliot wrote and delivered lectures for Corpus Christi College Cambridge on *The Idea of a Christian Society*. In their Faber-published form, Eliot, in his Introduction, acknowledged the influence both of Christopher Dawson's ideas and of the detailed comment and criticism given to his draft by George Every.

However, these inputs had in reality been considerably more extensive. Canon Strudwick recalls[44] that Eliot had discussed the entire draft content of these lectures beforehand throughout Kelham, amongst all the brethren and the students, and in particular with Fr. Gabriel Hebert there (and naturally with George Every).

It is tempting simply to see the spiritual *Weltanschauung* of Nicholson himself as derived from the thought of his direct and indirect mentors, such as Dawson (via George Every); from Every himself and from Eliot etc. To an extent, this seems entirely plausible: Dawson's view of all civilisations through past ages having been underpinned by religious principles and all having been part of a common cycle of birth, growth, flourishing, decline and eventual death, with successive new ones being born out of the remains of the old does indeed reflect much of Nicholson's (and, perhaps, Eliot's) *credo.* Nicholson seems to have accepted this concept as absolutely implicit to all of life on earth, in both its physical and sociological aspects.

Nicholson became intensely interested in the developing lay theology of Charles Williams[45], who was well-acquainted with George Every, but, curiously, whom Nicholson probably never actually met. The Charles Williams Society Archives in Oxford hold a letter from Williams to Every dated 22nd July 1943 in which Williams thanks Every for letting him know that Nicholson had recently been very ill.[46] Williams adds that he and Nicholson had never actually met, although they had corresponded: Nicholson always with great courtesy and interest in Williams' *Taliessin* work.

In another letter, Williams mentions his pleasure at his own work (both poems and religious drama extracts) having been included by Nicholson in his *Anthology of Religious Verse*[47]. Nicholson's early affinity for Every's work too is evident from the fact that he included no less than four Every poems in the same Anthology.

Every himself abandoned faith in Anglo-Catholicism for Roman Catholicism when Kelham was closed down in 1973 and he moved to St. Mary's College, Oscott, the Seminary of the Roman Catholic Archdiocese of Birmingham, living and teaching there until his death, aged ninety-four, in 2003 (hence of course Canon Strudwick's allusion, above, to 'Oscott').

George Every was one of the many mourners who attended Nicholson's funeral in 1987 even though Every himself was by then seventy-eight years of age.

Before he died, Every met with an Australian academic, Dr Barry Spurr, primarily to discuss Every's connections with T.S. Eliot. This information, along with further data supplied by Mary Trevelyan, formed the basis of a recently published study by Dr Spurr of T.S. Eliot's Christianity[48]. Dr Spurr's personal impressions[49] of Every are interesting: he perceived him to have been a particularly delicate and exceedingly sensitive person. This may explain Every's shadowy profile, but his profound influence on Nicholson throughout Nicholson's entire life is plain, despite the deliberate destruction of most of the related evidence, this being their respective collections of their voluminous private interpersonal correspondence.

These acts of destruction must have amounted to nearly every single letter that had been exchanged between the two of them. All were deliberately destroyed as a result of a rather extraordinary pact that Every and Nicholson agreed during the 1980s, in order, they had discussed, to deprive any future academic researchers of possible source material. Fortunately, Gardner, in the course of his own, earlier (1970) thesis had been granted access to virtually all of this same correspondence, both from Every's side and from Nicholson's too. Gardner's thesis extensively quotes from all this body of subsequently-destroyed letters and Gardner's references now constitute the only surviving, albeit partial, record of it all.

This drastic act of mutual destruction probably took place around 1984, but this can only be surmised from the content of the only surviving reference to it - the actual letter between them discussing the plan has fortuitously escaped destruction[50] but is undated.

In addition to his strong T.S. Eliot connections, George Every interacted extensively with many other prominent members of the literary establishment over several decades from the 1930s until about the 1960s, his close contacts including Michael Roberts and his wife, Janet Adam Smith.

For just one notable example of these wide associations, during the 1940s and early 1950s, Every lectured at St Anne's House, Soho, where there was a flourishing outreach centre, which had been established in order to link the clergy and church laity with the literati of the day. On the literary side, some of its active members and supporters included T.S. Eliot, Dorothy L. Sayers, Charles Williams and of course George Every.

St Anne's House had been founded in 1942 by two Anglo-Catholic priests, Patrick McLaughlin and Gilbert Shaw, the Priest in Charge of St Anne's with the aim of putting thinking non-believers in touch with Christianity. Dorothy L. Sayers was a close friend of McLaughlin, and a driving force behind obtaining the permission of the Bishop of London to sanction the entire project.

In similar fashion to how the Student Christian Movement's Swanwick Conferences were organised, St Anne's House invited speakers to deliver programmes of lectures on apposite specialist subjects. The theme of the very first series of lectures was *Christian Faith and Contemporary Culture*; these started in the summer of 1943. T.S. Eliot spoke on Literature, Dorothy L. Sayers on Drama, the Director of the Victoria and Albert Museum on the Visual Arts, Lady Rhondda (proprietor and patron of *Time and Tide magazine*) on journalism and The Rev Dr James Welch, BBC Head of Religious Broadcasting, on broadcasting.

St Anne's House must have had enthusiastic support from some key staff of *The Church Times,* for this newspaper gave out notices for forthcoming lectures in its editorial material, rather than in the usual paid-for advertising. In 1950, the newspaper reported that Dorothy L. Sayers had lectured before a large audience on *Dante: The Four Ways of Interpreting the Divina Commedia.* Also that a series of lectures on the work of Charles Williams had been arranged: in one such lecture Brother George Every spoke on the novels of Williams. Other speakers included John Heath-Stubbs, Anne Ridler, the Rev. P. McLaughlin and Norman Nicholson himself. Sadly, though, no material related to St Anne's House survives amongst Nicholson's papers.

By 1952, a series of 'Literary Conversations' was being promoted at St Anne's House. These were led by John Betjeman, Frances Cornford, Gerard Hopkins, Derek Patmore, Kathleen Raine and the Earl of Birkenhead, along with Alan Pryce-Jones, Edmund Blunden, Harold Nicolson and Osbert Lancaster. In 1954 *The Masque of the Manuscript* and *the Masque of the Perusal* by Charles Williams, with music by Hubert Foss, were performed over a three-day run. And, later in the year, there followed a course of lectures on *Image, Meaning and Metaphor*. Lecturers included: William Empson, Kathleen Raine, E. W. P. Tomlin, Margaret Braithwaite, Dr R. D. Scott, Sir Arthur Bliss, Matyas Seiber, Paul Hamburger, Sir Herbert Read, Eric Newton and Patrick Heron. Yet another series of lectures was planned on the topic of *The Shape of Work to Come*.

George Every's former university tutor Christopher Dawson supported the work of St Anne's House too, as did the popular 'whodunnit' detective story author, Agatha Christie (1890-1976).

In 1957, McLaughlin resigned from his post at St Anne's House of Director / Warden, and by 1958 the project finally closed down. Whether or not it had succeeded fully in its purpose as a 'missionary outpost for intellectual non-believers', it had certainly encouraged a diverse and distinguished group of people to collaborate in altruistic and evangelistic spirit, if only as regards their individual specialisms, enthusiasms and disciplines. It stands as further evidence of the extensive 'networking' which took place within these literary circles, even extending to the participation of faraway Nicholson, doubtless greatly aided and encouraged by George Every.

Nicholson must have been firmly committed to the St Anne's project to the extent that he was willing to undertake the long and, to him, very arduous journey from Millom to London, in order to participate in the activities at St Anne's, Soho.[51] However, it is intriguing that no trace of this remains in his surviving papers: possibly this is further indication of Nicholson's highly selective document-retention practices.

3.03 Michael Roberts and Janet Adam-Smith

Michael Roberts (1902–1948) was a gifted scholar, teacher and author, who originally took university degrees in Chemistry and Mathematics (London and Cambridge respectively) and subsequently became a school teacher. In 1935, he married Janet Buchanan Adam-Smith (1905–1999), who was to become a significant literary figure in her own right. During the 1930s, Roberts met T.S. Eliot, who, at Faber and Faber, published Roberts's poetry and the two of them became good friends.

George Every also became firm friends with Roberts and his family, and, as already outlined, it was through Every that Norman Nicholson's early poetry first came to the attention of Michael Roberts.

In 1939, Newcastle Royal Grammar School, where Roberts taught, was evacuated to Penrith in Cumbria and Roberts and his family moved there temporarily. They lived at first at 49a Wordsworth Street, and when their friend, the poet and academic Kathleen Raine, left her then-husband, Charles Madge, they invited her and her children to live with them in Penrith. In summer 1940, the owners of the Wordsworth Street property wanted to sell it, so the Roberts family moved to The Garth, Arthur Street in Penrith, and Kathleen Raine and children moved out into the nearby country, to Martindale Vicarage, a very isolated place overlooking Ullswater, where she lived with her children for about 18 months, and where she completed most of her first collection of poetry, *Stone and Flower.*

Michael Roberts became employed by the BBC's European Broadcasting Service in London, in summer, 1941, and he moved to digs in Notting Hill Gate, whilst Janet and the children remained in Penrith. At the end of the War, Michael was appointed Principal of the College of St. Mark and St John, Chelsea, and in July, 1945 his family moved from Penrith to join him in London, where he died aged only forty-six, in 1948, as a result of leukaemia.

Norman Nicholson became a close family friend of the Roberts's.[52] In 1942, Nicholson visited Janet and the children at Arthur Street,[53] where a conversation with the then-four-year-old Andrew Roberts inspired one of Nicholson's best-known and most anthologised poems, *Rising Five,*[54] as well as another in *Five Rivers - For Hokey* (Andrew's nickname) and Henrietta[55] (who was Andrew's sister, born 1939). Another son, Edward Adam Roberts[56], had been born at The Garth in 1940. Adam's godparents were T.S. Eliot and Helen Sutherland. Janet Adam-Smith herself was a devoted godmother to Kathleen Raine's daughter (born 1934),Anna Madge (now Anna Hopewell).[57]

The infant Andrew Roberts, having 'risen five' started primary school in Penrith, in September, 1942.[58]

Many assorted Roberts' family friends and associates visited The Garth during this wartime period, including George Every, whose monk's habit greatly fascinated the Roberts's children.

In 1947, just a year before his father's untimely death, the Roberts's third son, John, was born.

Janet Roberts, or Janet Adam Smith as she was professionally known, returned from Penrith to London, at the end of the War, and was Assistant Literary Editor of the *New Statesman*, from 1949 to 1952, then Literary Editor there until 1960. In 1965, she married John Dudley Carleton (1908-1974), who was Head Master at Westminster School between 1957 and 1970. Janet was the author and editor of several books: *Mountain Holidays*, a travel classic of its period, was written in Penrith, during World War II. She produced accomplished biographies and studies of Robert Louis Stevenson, Henry James and of John Buchan, and edited several collections of poetry. She received an honorary Doctorate of Letters from the University of Aberdeen in 1962 and was awarded the O.B.E. in 1982.

Janet's second husband was a far more conventional figure than Michael Roberts had been. For example, Michael had once been tasked with teaching physics and the concepts of laws of motion and gravity to young boys, which he tackled by explaining to them why, shake things as much as they could, boys often experienced a wet trickle down the leg after a trip to the toilet.[59] Inspired, innovative, teaching, and perhaps not at all unacceptable in 2014, but such an approach did not at all endear him to the stuffier personages amongst head teachers of over half a century ago.

Coincidentally, but nonetheless interestingly, the family of Janet Adam Smith was fairly distantly related to that of Nicholson's contemporary Cumbrian poet, Margaret Beatrice Cropper.[60] Indeed, it is suggested by the source of this snippet of information that this kind of 'coincidence' simply stands as testimony to the propensity of the Victorians to marry their cousins.

3.04 Samuel Taylor

Sam Taylor (1884–1956) was born in the parish of Cartmel, Cumbria and was educated at Charterhouse and at Trinity College, Cambridge. He was vicar of nearby Flookburgh from 1916 to 1926 and later moved to incumbencies in

Carlisle (1926), Fallowfield in Manchester (1931), to Millom (with Kirksanton and Hill Chapel) (1935), and finally to Burneside, near Kendal (1944). He retired to live near his native Cartmel in 1949. His interests included research into his (patrician) ancestors, the Lamplugh and Irton families, once prominent landowners in West Cumberland, although he was one of a long line of Samuel Taylors who came originally from Moston, near Manchester. He wrote the still-standard work on the history of the Parish, *Cartmel, People and Priory*, which was first published shortly before his death. He had served as a military chaplain in France during World War One, where he was wounded.

Taylor was a highly-cultured individual and a fervent Socialist. He was a relative of Aldous Huxley and one of his friends was Kurt Hahn, the founder of Gordonstoun School, who once offered Taylor the post of Gordonstoun School Chaplain, which Taylor declined.

The Rev. (later Canon) Taylor was incumbent of Millom's 'old' church, Holy Trinity, and, via Bessie Satterthwaite, became a lifelong friend, sounding board and general mentor to Norman Nicholson as well as the archetype for the *Canon Olds* character of Nicholson's (1959) book *Provincial Pleasures.*[61]

In an obituary in *The Church Times*[62] Nicholson recalled that he had first known Sam Taylor not just as the parson, but as the Millom man with books to lend to youngsters like himself: Nicholson himself had possessed very few books but had a voracious appetite for devouring all manner of them, especially everything modern. Sam Taylor's house became something of an unofficial youth centre, where earnest discussions took place, not confined to matters of religion, but often covering social and economic issues. This was the height of the 1930s Depression: Sam Taylor's socialism and social conscience possibly rubbed off onto the young Nicholson and helped shape his future outlook in this regard.

3.05 Enrica Garnier

Enrica Garnier (1911-1991) was Nicholson's first serious female companion, and the fascinating story of her life is recounted here at fairly considerable length, simply because it deserves to become better-known, both in connection with the life and works of Norman and indeed in its own right.

Their relationship was described in some detail by Gardner in his original PhD thesis, but, curiously, all but perfunctory mention of Enrica was omitted from Gardner's subsequently published book on Nicholson[63]. One might speculate that Gardner's thesis had not been subject to quite the same formal and tacit sanctions and permissions as were necessary for a published book, and Nicholson, who was by then happily married to Yvonne, may well have exercised some influence over the content.

This being a critical biography, and not subject to similar constraints, a considerably fuller story can now be told, which it is hoped will serve somewhat to rectify this significant omission.

(Jessie)[64] Enrica Garnier was Nicholson's first serious girlfriend, from around 1937 until at least the mid-1940s. She and Nicholson had first met via John Edward Fisher who was later to become Head of English at Mexborough Grammar School near Rotherham in South Yorkshire. There, Fisher had first recognised and later nurtured the exceptional poetic talents of one of his sixth formers, namely, the young Ted Hughes.

During the late 1930s, Nicholson and Enrica spent holidays together, along with Fisher and other friends.[65]

Enrica was born to European Baptist Church missionary parents, in Tai Yuanfu, Northern China, and spent her early years there. Her mother had grown up in Blackheath, London and was the daughter of a grocer. She was of deep religious faith, and, by the turn of the century, she had resolved to go to China as a missionary, where she met Albert Garnier.

Albert Garnier was a French-speaking Italian Protestant. His father had been the Director of the Waldensian College in Pellice, northern Italy. The Waldensians are a minority religious group, who during the 17th century, were forced to flee from intense and barbaric Roman Catholic persecution. Many fled across the mountains into France, taking refuge along the way in the rocks and the caves.

'For the might of thine arm we bless thee' was a hymn written by this persecuted group and it was adopted by the Garnier family as their personal hymn. Albert's mother was widowed early in life, and had singlehandedly to provide for her family on a tiny income, but she ensured

that her children received as good an education as was possible, given the circumstances. Albert was her elder son (born 16 June, 1881), and he became an evangelist whilst still a student, walking considerable distances across the local mountains to preach in many of the outlying villages. He too had felt a calling to become a missionary, so, in order to fund his training, he took menial work in a Turin boot factory. He later obtained a college place in England to train for the Baptist Ministry. One of his many talents was the ease with which he could become fluent in other languages: he spoke French, Italian, English and Mandarin Chinese. After retiring from his missionary work, he became Pastor of the Huguenot Church in Canterbury and worked as a linguist for the BBC.[66]

Enrica was schooled in Northern China from the age of 8 until she was 13, at the American Board Mission School, Tungchow[67] then, in 1925, she was enrolled at Walthamstow Hall School in Sevenoaks, Kent, a (still, in 2014, flourishing and prestigious) boarding school, established specifically for the daughters of Christian overseas missionaries.[68] Although denied a British student maintenance grant because her father was of Italian nationality, Enrica subsequently trained as a teacher at Homerton College Cambridge from 1930 to 1932. Homerton, although non-denominational at the time, was an institution with very strong nonconformist connections. Enrica's training at Homerton reflected this tradition, and focused upon close study of English Literature.

Enrica's first teaching appointment was in August 1932, at Claremont Avenue School, Kenton, Middlesex, where she taught classes of up to forty-nine pupils.[69] In August 1936, she left to take up a post nearby, at East Lane Junior School, Wembley. Notes relating to Enrica are still retained in the Kenton School's files and read thus:

> *She has done excellent work especially in English, and Swimming. Her discipline was very good and her manner bright and cheerful. She leaves to gain other experience.*[70]

In 1936, Enrica changed her teaching post again, this time going far outside London, north to the Sheffield area, where she first met John Edward Fisher and, through him, Norman Nicholson himself. In 1937, Enrica joined the teaching staff of her old school, Walthamstow Hall, where she remained for the next 34 years, retiring in 1972. She specialised in teaching French and Religious Knowledge.

As a consequence of severe bombing damage in the Blitz[71] to the main school in Sevenoaks, the junior boarders and some junior day girls were evacuated well away from this vulnerable and dangerous area, and from November 1940 until November 1944, they occupied Pontesford House, a large Victorian house on the outskirts of the village of Pontesbury, about eight miles south-west of Shrewsbury in Shropshire.

Enrica was appointed teacher in charge at Pontesford House, and Nicholson regularly visited her there, taking the long train journey from Millom. His fine poem, *September in Shropshire* reflects one such visit, whilst another poem from *Five Rivers*, entitled *Coastal Journey* probably does so too. *Five Rivers* was Nicholson's first volume of poetry, and was published by Faber and Faber in 1944. The book is dedicated to Enrica, who had spent countless hours preparing the typescript, and in the process having to decipher Nicholson's almost illegible handwriting.

Earlier, in 1938, Nicholson had visited London, where he and Enrica were granted an audience with T.S. Eliot at the Faber offices in Russell Square. Eliot's assistant at the time was the poet and playwright Anne Ridler, who recalled shortly before her death her high regard for Nicholson and his poetry, and how she had looked after Norman's 'fiancé' whilst he was in the great man's presence.[72] Anne Ridler was of course mistaken in assuming that the couple were engaged to be married, but this is indicative of just how very close their relationship must have seemed at that time.[73]

In 1939, Nicholson attended the Student Christian Movement's Swanwick Conference as a Lecturer / Seminar Leader, alongside other distinguished speakers such as Moelwyn Merchant, C.S. Lewis and John Betjeman. Norman stayed for the full week of the Conference as a guest of the S.C.M., whilst Enrica herself came for a one-night stay, in accommodation for which she paid seventeen shillings (eighty-five pence in modern decimal currency).[74]

Enrica was to become friends in her own right with many literary contacts of Nicholson, particularly with George Every[75], with Kathleen Raine,[76] and with Anne Ridler. There is surviving evidence that Enrica accompanied Nicholson on his visits to Helen Sutherland at Cockley Moor.[77] Enrica also once visited Nicholson on his home ground in Millom, and met his father and stepmother, but her own mother in London suffered a sudden illness and her stay had to be cut short as a result.[78]

The young schoolgirls who were evacuated to Pontesford House seventy years ago are all elderly ladies now, but unanimously, and touchingly, regard the whole experience (as well as Enrica's influence) as one of the happiest occasions in their entire lives. They praise copiously, for instance, Enrica's almost-saintly dedication and enthusiasm and her inspirational teaching methodology. This is an extract from one of Enrica's regular despatches to Walthamstow Hall from Pontesford[79], quoted at almost full length because the delight experienced by all involved in this isolated little community - and indeed much of Enrica's own personality – is so lucidly described and is absolutely palpable:

> *...it was the summer days we will none of us ever forget. Directly after lunch, with knapsacks packed in the intervals of study, practising and mending, off we all went - an unspeakable collection to look at. Nearly always it was to Happy Valley. There, between steep wooded sides, was a shallow, busy stream, with the right sort of rocks and stones, clay banks for making pots, fallen trees for canoes, and simply no dangers for any child over three, except of getting wet. On the hottest days we bathed but nowhere was deep enough for swimming. Beyond Happy Valley was the Land of Bumpy Moss,*

at its best in February. Once the older ones followed a disused single track railway line which had worked the material of a barytes mine in the past, until we came to a beautiful field full of flowers looking over to the Welsh Hills. It was someone's birthday and we all wore garlands for tea, and ran about barefoot and found orchids none of us knew. Some were sent to Miss Mitchell in a matchbox and pronounced to be Greenwing Orchids, and not very common. I remember thinking that the scene was not unlike the fields of Enna where Persephone played with her friends among the flowers.

We saw a number of unusual things, one time or another. We found a white owl, dazed in a wood, and he was brought home, perched on a stick, to live some days in a shed before leaving. A gold-crested wren flew into a bedroom and allowed everyone to see him well. He sat in my hand like warm thistledown, heart rather hammering, but with an unalarmed bright eye, before he flew away. A squirrel pressed his nose against the big schoolroom window. A hedgehog went for a long slow walk across our grass. There were any number of nuthatches and a kingfisher by Bore's Mill. The wood opposite had a great variety of fungi, and Shining Cranesbill[80] *grew around the Hill…*

Further recollections kindly supplied by Enrica's evacuees and her many family and Walthamstow Hall friends warmly confirm with penetrating and touching fluency the sweetness and sincerity of Enrica's nature. A few examples:

Enrica's imagination responded to everything our situation at Pontesford had to offer: a flexible time-table, space out of doors and the opportunity to learn from Shropshire itself. I remember acting appropriate scenes in Ludlow Castle (history), taking note of the igneous rocks on Pontesford Hill (geography), joining in our own Eisteddfod (poetry and music). Enrica's methods were often ahead of her time. She was also rigorous and practical. She set and corrected umpteen written exercises. Vocabulary tests; spelling bees; learning by heart, a composition entitled "How to clean a pair of shoes", all figure in my memory.

Enrica's emotional spontaneity was expressed mainly in 'whooshing' feelings for nature; religion; love of humanity; children....she was engaging, joyful in an almost childlike way and often almost eccentric – even flirtatious, but not in any sexy or sensual way...

At Pontesford she turned many things to magic - poetry; Lorna Doone; the local countryside; French songs; creating and acting plays, or Shakespeare on the lawn; serenading a local writer on her birthday with 'Morning has broken'...

...her teaching is still alive: and so it deserves to be, for it was truly "alive" then...

(From a former Walthamstow Hall pupil,
and, later, Head Mistress)

Others comment upon how exceptionally pretty Enrica looked, just like a teenager when in reality a young woman in her late twenties.

Enrica had all her stored papers destroyed by burning in the 1980s (possibly upon hearing news of Nicholson's death)[81], so none of her correspondence survives, nor much of the poetry she herself wrote.

But, one of Enrica's poems, about her father's home in Northern Italy, has, fortunately, survived:

La Fornasa

The house lies under the snow
And under the snow
Lie the steep fields where the ski-runners go.
Those slopes in summer, soft with dizzy gold
Now shine as white as Christmas in the Alpine cold.

Under the snow lie all our summer days
The laughter and the loving lazy ways.
The mid-day courtyard, and the food and wine
Where grew the lemon tree
And the old vine;
And when the meal was done
The long siesta in the sun.

Under the summer lies the snow.
Thus sequence and consequence seem to go
But in the integrity beyond our sun,
Summer and snow exist as one.

It seems, though, that the young Enrica's personal life had not been without its difficulties. Available and concrete details are sparse, but she had during this time become very attached to a London journalist, whom she was apt to refer to as 'My dear Hack[82]'. Unknown to Enrica and her journalist friend until many years later, Enrica's mother had learned of the relationship and had taken drastic but successful action to stop it.[83] At least one informant has recalled, too, that the relationship was rekindled, albeit very briefly, after Enrica and Nicholson broke up their romance.

The reasons for the breakup of such an intense and seemingly idyllic relationship as existed between Enrica Garnier and Norman Nicholson are cloaked in mystery: little or no evidence survives, so there can only be conjecture and speculation. Some who were close to Enrica, and to Nicholson, might consider that both of the former couple took great pains to keep these reasons private, and that their wishes should therefore be respected. Certainly, this study has no wish to disregard their (albeit posthumous) rights to privacy, so this matter must for now remain under wraps.[84] We shall therefore stick to the facts, which are, that, by 1946, the available evidence is that the former relationship was over; Enrica and Norman went their separate ways, she teaching in Sevenoaks and he authoring in Millom.

Enrica remained in close contact with Anne Ridler and her family. Amongst her very many godchildren was Anne Ridler's daughter, Kate. Enrica had meantime become friendly with the Sackville-West family at 'the big house' at Knole, near Sevenoaks; in fact four of the Sackville-West daughters had attended Walthamstow Hall School. Enrica is recalled by some who knew her as having been a regular visitor to Knole, possibly in order to deliver private tuition, but this connection cannot be fully verified via present Sackville-West family members' recollections. Kate Sackville-West does well recall Enrica as having been her own somewhat buttoned-up school teacher and, outside school, a friend of her mother. Kate's mother was Jacobine, who had married Lionel, the Sixth Baron Sackville, in 1953 and had died from cancer in 1971. Jacobine herself had literary leanings, having previously published three novels under the name of Jacobine Hitchens, and she had been researching a biography of a Sackville-West family member until shortly before she died. It is entirely plausible therefore that she and Enrica actively shared and exchanged literary interests.

Enrica never married, and she died in 1991.

It must be added that at least one source who knew Enrica very well recalls that she had been devastated by the break-up, Nicholson having hitherto proclaimed to her that he did not feel able to marry, but if he ever did so, it would be to Enrica. It must therefore have been doubly hurtful to Enrica that Nicholson ultimately did marry another, (Yvonne Gardner in 1956).[85]

It is noteworthy that Nicholson put up such a dense smokescreen about such a momentous event in his own personal life. Nearly all traces of Enrica were systematically excised, presumably by Nicholson himself, from his surviving personal papers.[86] It is almost inconceivable that an exceedingly literate couple in such an intense romantic relationship, but separated geographically by some considerable distance, did not correspond a lot, yet no trace of any correspondence remains. *The New Statesman* of 28th September 1946 did however publish an uncharacteristically ambiguous Nicholson poem entitled *Lullaby* which Gardner, in his thesis,[87] states was inspired by the break-up with Enrica This particular poem never subsequently appeared in any published collections of Nicholson's poetry, nor do any further surviving Nicholson poems appear to be attributable to this event.

Lullaby is a loose sonnet of a poem: just fourteen short lines, along an alliterative theme of 'Lying lonely, love', with intense images of blundering, and of desperate seeking and reaching-out, but finding nothing. The underlying theme observes the subject ('my Love's) loneliness and the reciprocal loneliness and groping for explanation on the part of the speaker. One cannot help but speculate whether or not any ambiguity exists in the deployment of the key word 'lie' – i.e. , in the sense of bodily repose and / or that of untruthfulness? For example, the final two lines:

> *Lie lonely, love*
> *Yet, lonely love, lie lightly.*

It is noteworthy, too, that there is evidence that further contact, at least of some kind, existed between Nicholson and Enrica up until at least 1948. Nicholson's topographical book *Cumberland and Westmorland* was published in 1949 and so probably was written during the preceding year (or before). It contains, in the 'Acknowledgements' Frontispiece, thanks to 'Miss Garnier' for typing-up the manuscript from handwritten material which Nicholson cheerfully admits therein was both lengthy and illegible.

Whether or not the couple again briefly became reconciled after the 1946 breakup, or simply kept some kind of non-romantic relationship going thereafter remains a matter for speculation. Certainly the loving, intimate dedication of 'To Enrica' in *Five Rivers* contrasts poignantly with the later, distant stiff formality of thanks to 'Miss Garnier', and Enrica herself may well have had very mixed feelings when she read this faint and formal praise in print: we shall probably never know for sure.

It is interesting, though, regarding this 'Enrica smokescreen', that, when being asked directly by the media about his life following the end point of *Wednesday Early Closing* and after his return to Millom from Linford, Nicholson was adamant that this period in his life had been absolutely uneventful to the point of being unworthy of any particular note.[88] Thus he really does seem to have thrown as heavy a veil as he possibly could over events in his personal life between the end of World War II and his meeting Yvonne Gardner, culminating with Yvonne becoming his wife in 1956.

Although she herself was seventy-six years of age in 1987, when Nicholson died, Enrica made the long journey to Cumbria in order to pay her final respects. One of Enrica's friends feels that Enrica never quite abandoned the hope that Nicholson would one day send for her, after their break-up, but, apart from the mystery of the c.1948 book manuscript, there is no evidence of any further post-separation contact between the estranged couple.

3.06 John Edward Fisher

John Edward Fisher (1914–1980) was a Millom schoolmate of Nicholson's who had left the town to study English at university and subsequently became a teacher at Mexborough Grammar School in South Yorkshire, where he remained for the whole of his teaching career.

Nicholson's letters to Sylvia Lubelsky mention Fisher bringing home a girl he had met at university, and on another occasion Nicholson's cousin, ('Sadie') falling in unrequited love with the vacationing Fisher.

Mexborough Grammar School was (as already mentioned) the *alma mater* of Ted Hughes, whose talent soon came to Fisher's recognition. Emory University, in Atlanta, USA, preserves the inscribed book given to Hughes by Fisher on the occasion of Hughes 'going up' to read English at Cambridge University, in 1951.

Fisher is still fondly remembered by many Mexborough Grammar alumni as a highly dedicated and inspirational teacher. But it was whilst he was himself still at university in 1934 that he shared with Nicholson a pivotal experience of T.S. Eliot's poetry, particularly *The Waste Land*.

Nicholson recalled this momentous occasion many times during his life, such as in 1948, as part of a contribution to a symposium of commentary on Eliot[89], in his piece entitled *Words and Imagery*. It was a hot summer day, he recounts, when 'a friend' had called for Nicholson, holding a copy of Eliot's early poems, beginning with *Prufrock* and ending with *The Hollow Men*, which they had persuaded Millom Library to acquire. Nicholson comments that his only impressions of Modernist poetry hitherto had been of somewhat meaningless assemblages of seemingly random jumbles of words. Eliot's deployment of words came as a total revelation, such that Nicholson subsequently immersed himself in *The Waste Land* poem, and with everything connected with it, such as Frazer's *Golden Bough*.

Many years later, in the course of a BBC local radio interview, Nicholson identified Fisher as the 'friend' involved, and noted in detail and with evident pride the Ted Hughes connection. Nicholson also attributed to this incident the changing of the entire course of his future life, being inspired henceforth to become a writer himself: furthermore, as a result of reading such as Frazer's observations about the pattern and cycles of the human world's religions and beliefs, Nicholson had been led towards the abandonment of his former atheism.

Jones' biography only briefly mentions the cricket field incident and not as at all pivotal. It was Sylvia Lubelsky, according to Jones, who introduced Nicholson to Eliot's poetry by sending him published copies. But, a former teaching colleague of Fisher at Mexborough Grammar still vividly remembers that Millom cricket field encounter as being one of Fisher's favourite and oft-repeated Eliot / Nicholson anecdotes.

Fisher was (as mentioned earlier) instrumental in Nicholson first meeting Enrica. Fisher became a keen motorist with a particular penchant for Citroen cars. Gardner's thesis relates an incident when Nicholson and Enrica were being driven by Fisher through one of the poorest and most deprived parts of the slums of Sheffield, and Norman being very deeply moved and greatly humbled by the abject poverty he witnessed so very closely – in fact separated from it only by the car's flimsy windows.

During World War II, Fisher had served as a Royal Navy Officer, on Atlantic convoy operations.[90]

Fisher died in 1980, from lung cancer. Ted Hughes had always kept in touch with Fisher and his family, and Hughes himself described Fisher's final illness in a letter to Harold Massingham[91]. In another letter, to Nick Gammage, dated 28th July 1993[92], Hughes mentioned that Nicholson had been Fisher's schoolmate in Millom, and, when Hughes was about seventeen years of age (i.e. in about 1947), Fisher had sent to Nicholson some examples of the young Hughes' poetry for his opinion. Nicholson had been impressed, Hughes recalls, but had warned him against unconsciously adopting the style of Dylan Thomas.[93]

Nicholson dedicated his (1975) autobiography *WEC* to Fisher, incorporating a little humorous dig to the effect that this act would provide another thing about which he could grumble.

Fisher had two daughters, Angela (b. 1943) and Frances (b. 1948). Frances died, very suddenly, from pneumonia, in 1969. Angela was able to supply details of her father's letters from Ted Hughes to Christopher Reid for his 2007 compilation of Hughes' letters. Angela herself is believed to have died in 2011.

3.07 Helen Sutherland (Cockley Moor) and her set

Helen Christian Sutherland (1881-1965) was a prominent patron of English modern art, music and literature, from the 1920s until her death. During the 1920s, she lived at Rock Hall, in Northumberland (and enthusiastically supported the Pitman Painters of Ashington[94]). There, she had first met Michael Roberts and his wife, Janet Adam Smith. She moved to Cockley Moor, a former farmhouse, high up in Matterdale, near Ullswater, in the northern English Lake District, in 1939. There she established and hosted a coterie of the literary and artistic *avant garde*, including David Jones, Winifred and Ben Nicholson, Barbara Hepworth, and Janet and Michael Roberts, via whom Kathleen Raine and her children became frequent visitors to Cockley Moor, and much-loved and supported by Helen herself.

Probably introduced in his own right by the Roberts'[95], Nicholson too became a regular visitor to Cockley Moor, from the early 1940s onwards. Unfortunately, little evidence survives of this aspect of Norman Nicholson's life, although the experience must have influenced his literary, cultural and social horizons, probably quite immensely. Nicholson's poem from *Five Rivers*, entitled *Cockley Moor* distils poetically his impressions of the house and of both its contents and its commanding setting[96]. There is evidence that Norman Nicholson himself owned a Ben Nicholson picture, which hung proudly, until the end of Norman's life, at 14 St. George's Terrace, and that both Enrica Garnier and Kathleen Raine regularly made the long train journey to Penrith from southeast England. Helen Sutherland's car - a Riley which had replaced her former big old Rolls Royce – must have had many runs from her eyrie overlooking Ullswater to Penrith Railway Station, in order to convey the frequent visitors to and from their trains.

One visitor was once T.S. Eliot, although his stopover destination was the home of the Roberts family, at The Garth in Penrith town. Janet Roberts much later in her life recalled[97] that Eliot first stayed with them in Penrith for one night, in Autumn 1941, in order to inspect his new godson, Adam Roberts (b. 1940) and again, in Summer, 1942, for two or three nights,[98] during which stay, he was conveyed, along with the Roberts's, by taxi to Cockley Moor in order to take tea with Helen Sutherland[99]. Helen had reacted thus:

> *...and who do you think was brought here by my long friends Janet and Michael Roberts one exquisite Sunday and ate some of my speciality of white currant jam? Well, T.S. Eliot. It moved me very much to meet him. He is beautiful to look at - very clear-cut features but so sensitively and generously moulded. I was so deeply struck*

> *by his humility and the extent of his humanity - I found, felt, or seemed to do so, what I did not at all expect or count on, an instinctive sympathy between us - though I was very shy and he is rather silent - so that I received something most special and lovely from his visit.*[100]

Other writers who visited Helen Sutherland at Cockley Moor included Margaret Cropper from Kendal and the poet Elizabeth Jennings.[101] Nicholson's own visits to Cockley Moor seem to have ended by around the end of World War Two. The reasons for this are not clear, but both Kathleen Raine and Michael and Janet Roberts had by then returned to homes in London, and Nicholson's relationship with Enrica Garnier had ended not long afterwards. A postcard from Kathleen Raine in London to Nicholson dated 1943 does survive in the Rylands Library[102]. Raine advises Nicholson therein that she 'lunched with Enrica' and proposes that they all meet up on a (specified) forthcoming date at Cockley Moor.

There is speculation in Jones' biography that there was some kind of romantic dimension to Norman's interaction with Kathleen Raine at Cockley Moor. To be sure, they were both fellow-poets, and, perhaps inevitably, influenced each other. Kathleen Raine then was a stunningly attractive woman, but no direct evidence whatsoever exists of any form of romantic feelings, on either side.

Enrica was Nicholson's close and loving companion throughout this period, accompanying him on at least some of his visits to Cockley Moor; indeed, Enrica was to become a friend in her own right of Kathleen Raine. Kathleen Raine's daughter, Anna Madge (b. 1934) was a very young child in the 1940s. Anna, looking back upon this early part of her life, recalls Nicholson quite well, but not with even an inkling of any unusual intensity in his relationship with her mother. There is no record of Kathleen Raine herself having mentioned Nicholson other than in passing and by name only in any of her published work or private correspondence. Anna recalls Nicholson coming to stay at her mother's Chelsea flat during the 1950s, but similarly recalls nothing otherwise unusual, other than that Nicholson had treated Anna (by then a teenager) with great charm and respect, and that her mother had seemed a little less irritated by Nicholson than was often the case with many other people with whom she interacted. Anna adds, though, that her mother still found Norman to be a rather tiresome person, and she describes the notion that Norman and her mother ever had any kind of relationship as "complete rubbish!"

Helen's birthday was once commemorated by a special presentation to her of a (1958) picture (*La Belle Endormie*) by David Jones.[103] On the back was an appreciative verse addressed to Helen, and the whole *verso* panel featured a collage of the signatures of Helen's many friends.[104] The picture is in a private collection, but images of the signatures on the back do not appear to include Nicholson's own, indicating perhaps that Nicholson's close involvement with the Cockley Moor set had by then ended. However, correspondence from Helen Sutherland dated 1965 survives in Nicholson's papers[105] which is indicative of a still-warm relationship between them. Helen for example invites Nicholson and Yvonne to come to stay with her. This is consistent too, with other sources which recount the eventful and eccentric life of the Cumbrian artist Percy Kelly (1918-1993) that, in 1960, Nicholson had sent a letter of recommendation and introduction relating to Kelly to Helen Sutherland, which had resulted in Kelly himself being invited to visit Cockley Moor.[106]

Percy Kelly became a regular correspondent with Nicholson. Although he was notoriously unwilling ever to sell any of his beloved paintings, Kelly was a prolific letter writer and was in the habit of carefully decorating letters to his special friends with profuse and colourful illustrations and calligraphy, all in his characteristic and unique style. Many of these remarkable little works of art fortunately have survived, and those sent from c.1971 until 1984 have been collated by Dr David A. Cross in a most attractive and interesting booklet.[107]

Cross's book refers to Kelly and Nicholson having first met in 1955, when Kelly was still the thirty-seven-year old Postmaster at Little Broughton, a West Cumbrian village near Cockermouth, and that they were introduced via Alan Freer (b. 1926)[108], himself an artist as well as a Manchester school inspector of English. Freer's own papers confirm that Nicholson was a regular contributor to Freer's regular initiatives, aimed at broadening and enriching the educational experiences of Manchester area school pupils and their teachers by bringing to their attention and direct experience the works of his extensive contacts amongst modern UK writers and artists.

Kelly had enrolled as a mature student at Carlisle (Cumberland) College of Art during the early 1960's, where a young Conrad Atkinson (b. 1940) from Cleator Moor - an ex-ore mining and iron making town in West Cumberland visited and written about by Nicholson - was a member of the same class and remembers Kelly well. Atkinson is presently a Professor of Art at the University of California at Davis, and is one of the world's leading contemporary painters. West Cumberland, (like Millom) being a very close-knit area, Atkinson recalls catching the school bus every day from Cleator Moor to Whitehaven Grammar School accompanied by a cousin of Nicholson, whose family had 'emigrated' from Millom to Cleator Moor. Atkinson also recalls Winifrid Nicholson, the artist and first wife of Ben Nicholson (who was not related to Norman) from his Art College days, remembering especially her very aristocratic aura.

Helen Sutherland was obliged by failing health finally to vacate her Cockley Moor home in 1965.[109] In 1972 the house was bought by the astrophysicist and science fiction writer, Sir Fred Hoyle (1915-2001) and the bands of visiting intellectuals returned to Cockley Moor, but this time with the world's top physicists having replaced the artists.

3.08 T.S. Eliot & Anne Ridler

T.S. Eliot's influence permeated the whole of Nicholson's life and work, as of course it did the whole of contemporary English Literature. As Eliot himself once identified as an inevitable literary phenomenon,[110] Eliot's own body of work has become an indelible part of twentieth-century literary tradition. An appropriate parallel can perhaps be drawn with Sigmund Freud's great influence upon psychology or that of John Maynard Keynes upon economics. Nicholson himself once observed[111] that long ago *The Waste Land* had represented a major part of the avant garde of poetry and that Eliot was then a newcomer who had not at that stage attained his subsequent, revered status within the literary congregations. The publication of *The Waste Land* was the beginning of a revolutionary process, which changed all that completely, both for Nicholson's *oeuvre* in micro terms and for the whole of English Literature, from the macro perspective. For Nicholson himself, the Eliotic revolution began momentously in the summer of 1934, when he and John Edward Fisher first encountered Eliot's early poetry, including *The Waste Land*. This event has already been recounted in detail so will not be repeated here.

In or about the same year of 1934, Anne Ridler (1912-2001) had obtained an editorial job at Faber and Faber. In 1935, Eliot's Secretary left her job, and Anne Ridler was appointed by Eliot to be his Secretary, a post which she held until 1940[112]. Anne Ridler was the daughter of a Housemaster at Rugby School who was also a poet and author; her mother too was the author of many popular children's books.[113]

Anne Ridler's own first poetry collection was published in 1939. In 1942, Nicholson included three of her poems in his Penguin *Anthology of Religious Verse*, so Nicholson may have first made Anne Ridler's acquaintance in connection with his early but nonetheless influential book. Both she and Nicholson wrote verse plays, some of which were staged by E. Martin Browne at the Mercury Theatre: Anne Ridler's *The Shadow Factory* was first performed in 1945, followed in 1946 by Nicholson's *Old Man of the Mountains.* Eliot, of course, had started the trend a decade earlier, with *The Rock* (1934) and *Murder in the Cathedral* (1935).[114]

3.09 E. Martin Browne

Integral to Chapter Nine – 'The Plays'

3.10 S.L. Bethell

Samuel Leslie Bethell (1908-1955) died at an inordinately young age: like Michael Roberts and Charles Williams, he was denied by a premature death the opportunity to develop his very considerable talents. Bethell was born in Workington, Cumbria (only about 45 miles from Nicholson's Millom), where his father was a banker. He went to school in Workington and married a schoolmate, Margaret (Morton) (always 'Madge' to her friends) in 1937.

He must have excelled at school, for he went on to study at Selwyn College, Cambridge, initially for ordination in the Church, but changing later to a degree in English. He progressed to a Doctorate of Letters and a lecturing post in the English Department of Cardiff University, where he taught Moelwyn Merchant (1913-1997) who in turn became a fellow lecturer at Cardiff before in 1961 being appointed Professor of English at Exeter University.

Nicholson, George Every and Bethell shared a strong personal friendship, and, indirectly, very many prominent literary and artistic friends and contacts, including for example T.S. Eliot, Moelwyn Merchant, R.S. Thomas and the sculptress Barbara Hepworth; Bethell thus served as yet another 'route focus' of all these points of contact and a further powerful illustration of a component of that pervasive and extensive web of literary and artistic networking which operated throughout the interwar years, then during World War Two and thereafter for almost the remainder of the 20th century. For just one random example: Barbara Hepworth connects firstly with Helen Sutherland and with Nicholson and all the Cockley Moor set, then later closely with Moelwyn Merchant and indirectly via Bethell back to Nicholson.

One might speculate that Bethell's rise to literary and academic prominence was cut short only by his premature death at just forty-seven, whilst Moelwyn Merchant in a sense assumed Bethell's mantle by default, at least in part, through living long enough to rise to senior academic status.

Bethell's influential book on Shakespeare and popular dramatic tradition[115] contained such a heartfelt and most-touching dedication to his late father that it deserves a verbatim mention here:

> *To my revered and beloved father* OLIVER BETHELL *who died on the first of January 1938* I DEDICATE THIS BOOK *in gratitude for his example of Christian life, and for the patient criticism and enthusiasm to which I owe in great measure whatever may be of value in my work. May God grant him perpetual light and peace.*

Bethell's *oeuvre* even though cut so tragically short was already quite extensive, including an early (pub. 1933) novel, *The Subtile* (sic) *Knot* and many books on Shakespeare studies as well as commentary upon individual plays (especially *The Winter's Tale*) along with literary criticism and some poetry too. Nicholson included no less than four poems by Bethell in his (1942) *Anthology of Religious Verse*, and Bethell probably often sought via their correspondence Nicholson's opinion on his latest poetry. Bethell usually visited his native West Cumberland for annual family holidays, during which he frequently met up with Nicholson

Bethell's first contact with T.S. Eliot was in 1934, when Eliot, in his capacity as Editor of *The Criterion* magazine provisionally accepted Bethell's submission of an article about I.A. Richards' Theory of Value and commented favourably upon the young Bethell's analysis thereof.

Further generally encouraging correspondence between Bethell and Eliot took place, during the next fifteen years or so. Despite being unwilling to commit Faber & Faber to publishing any of Bethell's work, Eliot was clearly personally impressed by it, to the extent of offering to use his influence with an alternative publisher. Eliot even went so far as to write a Foreword for Bethell's book on Shakespeare and the popular dramatic tradition, even though it was published by a rival firm.

Eliot's verse drama is discussed at length in connection with Nicholson's own verse plays, in Chapter Nine. But Eliot's interest in the tradition of verse drama generally and in Shakespearean drama in particular dated back to c. 1920.[116] Eliot then had addressed the question of why effective verse drama was no longer being written. He observed that, despite being popular entertainment, Shakespeare's drama had been in poetic form too and that the challenge of modern verse drama ought to be to make popular entertainment into a form of art, whilst retaining its qualities and functions as entertainment.

Now, in the 21st Century, contemporary verse drama is again not too often encountered, but Bethell's dramatic tradition study links with and illuminates considerably the bygone verse drama movement and the work of Eliot and his school (including, prominently, Nicholson within it. Bethell's ideas too seek to expose 'naturalistic' drama as limiting and spiritually bankrupt: a notion which Eliot and his followers would have applauded in their day, and one which is thought-provoking, even nowadays:

...Only the popular mind, as revealed in the popular theatre, preserved in crude melodrama something of the ancient wonder, and a sense that man is not in himself an adequate cause of his own remarkable history. On this, if on anything, the future of the drama – as of any social decency - must ultimately depend... [117]

A few years earlier than his study on dramatic tradition, Bethell published a classification and analysis of contemporary literature[118], as part of a series of 'Christian Newsletter' books, *'designed to assist thought upon the relevance of Christian faith to present problems'*, as the Series Editor's Preface put it. Other authors in the series already included George Every, with the *Christian Discrimination* book so scorned by F.R. Leavis. Bethell's, *'Literary Outlook'* book is similarly (but not nearly so rudely) critical of the work of Dylan Thomas, who was called by *The Listener's* Herbert Read one of 'the new romantics. But Bethell dismissed it quite scathingly:

...Isolation, the abandonment of meaning, and subsistence on an already almost exhausted deposit of nineteenth-century poetic language: these still seem to me to be the characteristics of Mr. Thomas and his friends...

It is not a new romantic movement, but the last stage in poetic dissolution...Our only hope of poetic continuity, then, lies in the Church... [119]

Bethell's views certainly do seem broadly to concur with those of George Every and Norman Nicholson: and (possibly or partially) even with those of T.S. Eliot. Moreover, in evaluating Nicholson's early poetry, Bethell's literary criticism cautiously but doggedly edged out onto a long limb:

> *....I am never prepared to prophesy in literary matters, but I believe that he (Nicholson) has already written some of the best poetry of his generation...*[120]

It is notable that Bethell's praise of Nicholson's early poetry even pre-dated the publication of *Five Rivers*, although some but not all of Nicholson's poems included in that collection had earlier been published piecemeal in periodicals. It is notable too, that Bethell used the words *'has already written'*: further support perhaps for the proposition that Nicholson's earliest work represented some of the best poetry of his entire *oeuvre*.

3.11 Yvonne Gardner

Yvonne Edith Gardner (1921-1982) married Norman in 1956, when she was aged thirty-five and he forty-two. She had as a child attended Rhodes Avenue Junior School and later Glendale Grammar School, Wood Green, London, where she achieved a high-level matriculation pass. In World War II she joined the WRNS as a 'Torpedo WREN'[121].

After the war she attended a Government Retraining Course for teaching. Her first post was in Ladywell, Birmingham where she lodged with the local Vicar and his wife, Norman and Sybil Darrall. She specialised in teaching Drama and Modern Dance.

When the Darralls moved to Millom, Yvonne accompanied them and obtained a secondary school English and Drama teaching post in the town. She was involved in many productions at her school, often herself laboriously sewing the many costumes involved.

As a result of attending a course in producing Drama, run by E. Martin Browne, Yvonne approached Norman in connection with producing an extract from Nicholson's verse play, *The Old Man of the Mountains*[122].

This contact, originally via one of Nicholson's visits to the Darralls at the Vicarage[123], eventually led to their marriage in July, 1956. Norman was said to be horrified at the prospect of having to wear a suit, and eventually found and wore for the occasion one of his father's.[124] The couple subsequently honeymooned at the Woolpack Inn, in nearby Eskdale.

Yvonne moved into 14 St. George's Terrace into a carer's as well as wifely role, Nicholson's health being still very frail. She learned to drive; they bought a car and Yvonne transported Norman on topographical research forays and to most of his engagements, including his many readings, both looking after him and assisting him with the readings of his work. Yvonne also became adept at reading Norman's atrocious handwriting and she thus learned effectively to edit his manuscripts.

A former (female) student at Millom school recalls the 'hilarious' (her own words) experience of Yvonne's obvious discomfiture whilst tutoring them about the facts of life during the 1960s.

Yvonne's sister's daughter (Liz)[125] now has Norman's much-cherished Queen's Gold Medal for Poetry. Her sister (Sarah) has inherited his O.B.E. Medal .

Yvonne was diagnosed with breast cancer in 1966; shortly afterwards, she was operated upon and was expected to have every chance of making a full recovery. Norman and Yvonne moved temporarily to the Vicarage at Wreay,[126] about five miles south of Carlisle in order to allow Yvonne to convalesce.[127] Their hosts were Nicholson's good friend, The Rev. James H. Eckersley and his wife, who was a trained nurse.[128]

Yvonne's subsequent cancer check-ups proved negative for many years; she returned to her teaching job, albeit on a part time basis.[129] Tragically, she developed secondary cancer, from which she died after a long illness, in 1982, at the age of sixty-one.

Nicholson buried a copy of his latest Faber-published poetry volume, *Selected Poems,* alongside Yvonne. He had dedicated it to her, and had been able to present it to her in published form just before she died. He prudently left room on Yvonne's tombstone for the inscription of his own name. Five years later, his mortal remains were reunited with Yvonne's within that grave in Millom Churchyard, overlooking his beloved cricket field.[130]

The early death of his wife hit Nicholson very hard indeed: her last three months of life had filled his own life with overwhelming purpose, but now he felt very alone and totally bereft. Fortunately, he had some domestic help[131] in the form of two of Yvonne's school former-students, who visited him regularly. One of Yvonne's former Millom School colleagues, Peggy Troll, befriended Norman and ensured that he could still access his engagements outside the town of Millom.

For many weeks following Yvonne's death, Nicholson was unable to find solace even in listening to his beloved music, but after about three months this handicap gradually diminished.[132]

3.12 Daniel Hay

Daniel Hay (1910–1980) was appointed Borough Librarian of Whitehaven in West Cumberland in 1933. He had intended to stay there just for two or three years for career development, but remained in Whitehaven for the duration of his working life. At the time of his appointment, Millom was an autonomous Rural District of Local Government. In 1974, Whitehaven Borough Council, Ennerdale Rural District Council (based at Cleator) and Millom R.D.C. all merged to form Copeland Borough Council which covered West Cumbria and parts of the Western Lake District from Millom in the south to Distington, about four miles south of Workington in the north and Wasdale Head and Eskdale in the east.

Irrespective of jurisdictional boundary lines, Daniel Hay soon developed a strong interest in the local history and the literary scene of the whole of West Cumberland, and as a result became acquainted with Nicholson in Millom. This relationship flourished over the years into a strong personal friendship. Daniel Hay become an enthusiastic admirer of Nicholson's works as well as an acute critic and commentator upon them.

Hay once confidently proclaimed:

> *No living Cumbrian has won such worldwide esteem as Nicholson. His books have been translated into French, Spanish, Portuguese, Norwegian, Danish and Welsh. He is by far the most outstanding writer that Cumberland has produced in the present century.*[133]

Hay, nearly fifty years ago, was another commentator who never regarded Nicholson's poetic development as a 'learning curve'. With the precision and veneration of a true bibliophile, he wrote:

> *'Five Rivers' has gone through several impressions. Of the three volumes of verse that he has published to date it is the one to which I return most often and most readily. That is not to imply that 'Rock Face' (Faber, 1947) and 'The Pot Geranium' (Faber, 1954) do not contain material of equal merit. The latter received the first recommendation of the then newly formed Poetry Book Society. It is just that for me 'Five Rivers' holds the key to what he will write later.*

'The Bow in the Cloud', one of the longer poems in it, foreshadows the new development that came when he wrote the first of his four verse plays, 'The Old Man of the Mountains' (Faber, 1946). This play opened Martin Browne's famous series of 'Plays by poets' at the Mercury Theatre. These have won for him a unique place among the playwrights of the present century.[134]

Ever the professional archivist, Hay kept a scrapbook of his personal correspondence with Nicholson, interspersed with press cuttings relating to Nicholson and his works from a cuttings agency as well as from his own sources.

It is interesting to note in the changing tone and content of this correspondence[135] the rapidly-thawing formality of the Nicholson - Hay relationship. The earliest letters[136] all begin stiffly (and of course now anachronistically) 'Dear Hay' and are signed-off 'Yours Ever, Nicholson, but the two soon become first-name chums, Nicholson habitually writing to him as 'Dear Dan' or 'My Dear Danny'.

These letters provide valuable miscellaneous insights into Nicholson's domestic and literary life, especially during the 1960s and 1970s, Yvonne Nicholson's breast cancer diagnosis and her resulting surgery in 1966 for example is relayed to Hay by Norman and is sympathetically discussed between them by correspondence. Yvonne's enforced absence from Nicholson's home for her operation in Whitehaven Hospital led to Nicholson's elderly stepmother being temporarily hospitalised and

Nicholson having briefly to leave their home, to be looked after at St. George's Vicarage, Millom.

It is probably yet another example of Nicholson's draconian culling of his personal papers that not one item of the Nicholson side of all the Daniel Hay correspondence has found its way into the Rylands Library holdings. Further evidence too, consequently, of the fact that, as extensive and expertly-catalogued as the Rylands holdings certainly are, they are by no means a full archive of Nicholson's entire correspondence or a complete picture of his life.

Hay was of exceptional help to Nicholson both as a researcher and as a publicist. Many lectures and similar events were organised over several decades for Nicholson in Whitehaven by Hay: for example, in June 1954, coinciding with the publication of Nicholson's third Faber Collection of Poetry, *The Pot Geranium*, a special exhibition was held in Whitehaven Public Library and opened by the Mayor. A contemporary newspaper report[137] paraphrased Nicholson's speech in response:

> *Mr Nicholson said the exhibition was a credit to the Library Committee and Mr Hay. Whitehaven had a special meaning for him, for it was one of the places connected with the beginning of his writing career. Whitehaven was the third word in the first poem published in a magazine in 1940.*[138] *Whitehaven, too, had been one of the anchor places behind his little spiritual pilgrimage.*

Mr Nicholson spoke of the intense 18th century vitality of West Cumberland, with its contrast of mines, sea, and countryside, a contrast which, at the same time, was a harmony. The exhibition, he concluded, made him feel that at least some people were trying to listen to him.

Does the closing paragraph, above, indicate that, during the 1950s, Nicholson felt generally rather ignored and side-lined as a poet? If so, this kind of feeling may have contributed to the very long 'block' from which his poetry output suffered between 1954 and 1972.

In 1969, Nicholson's topographical book, *Portrait of the Lakes* was published, this being a revamp and update of his much earlier Guide, (1949) *Cumberland and Westmorland*. Hay organised and hosted for this occasion a public Lecture by Nicholson in Whitehaven. In the preliminary correspondence, Nicholson mentioned that he no longer gave very many formal lectures, but favoured poetry readings, followed by impromptu discussions. He also explained that he was becoming rather hard of hearing; nonetheless, he was very confident indeed that he could hold the attention of an audience for over the hour or so envisaged.

Yvonne Nicholson accompanied Norman to the 1969 event, and ended it with a reading of Nicholson's (1941) poem, *Whitehaven*. The event appears to have been an entire success, although Nicholson later wrote to Hay that it had all made him very tired afterwards - further indication perhaps of his frail health.

It was Daniel Hay who hatched an ambitious plan during the early 1970s to confer great civic honour upon Nicholson. This preceded and perhaps anticipated in a bigger way, Copeland Council's decision, in 1984, to bestow upon Nicholson the honour of the first-ever Freeman of the Borough.

In 1973, Hay proposed in a letter to Nicholson that Copeland Borough Council might purchase Nicholson's little house at 14 St. George's Terrace, Millom and turn it into a museum in his honour. As compensation, the Council would provide Norman and Yvonne with a new bungalow, which would be far more modern and easier to live in.

It is hard to comprehend that the Councillors running such a workaday town and area as Whitehaven and its region would ever have agreed to fund such a project, and perhaps Nicholson sensed this[139], for he politely but firmly declined to take this any further. Nonetheless, Nicholson did complain that the low value of shop premises in Millom made him unable readily to afford to move to a property which may have fewer stairs and therefore prove more suitable for him in his old age, and asked Hay obliquely if he might possibly be able to use his contacts within the Council to assist.

In reality, Nicholson was being somewhat 'careful' with his money. Upon his death, in 1987, his estate was valued at nearly £216,000, which is equivalent to well over half a million pounds in 2014, so he could easily have afforded, without any external financial assistance, far more expensive housing than available at 14 St. George's Terrace. But, in proposing this ambitious plan at all, Hay may well have had confidence that he could win-over the local politicians to agree to it. However, Hay, perhaps was not so rash or impetuous ever to propose an impossible scenario. But, in any event, nothing came of it.

Daniel Hay was thus a staunch and longstanding friend to Nicholson, as well as being a willing and effective researcher for Nicholson's many and various topographical books and articles: both Nicholson's life and his local reputation would have been much the poorer without Hay's unstinting and generous input.

3.13 David Wright and Philippa Reid

This sub-chapter fast-forwards to a friendship in Nicholson's later life, beginning when he was an established poet and writer in his mid-fifties and ending shortly before his death in his early seventies. It may therefore seem incongruous to introduce it at this stage, but it was both a close and significant friendship, and a well-documented one, Nicholson's correspondence with the Wrights being preserved alongside Nicholson's own surviving papers, in the Manchester University John Rylands Library.

In spite of the potential chronological confusion, it is therefore included under this 'significant personae' grouping.

David Wright (1920-1994) was born in Johannesburg, South Africa He contracted scarlet fever when seven years old, which left him profoundly deaf for the rest of his life. He relocated to England at the age of fourteen and attended Northampton School for the Deaf and later Oriel College, Oxford, graduating in 1942.

Wright had the benefit of a modest private income. He became a freelance writer in 1947 after working on *The Sunday Times* for five years. He also co-founded and co-edited the quarterly literary review *X* from 1959 until 1962.

Wright co-wrote three books about Portugal with Patrick Swift, his co-founder and co-editor of *X*. His own reflections on his disability, *Deafness: A Personal Account* (1969) became an acclaimed and still well-known autobiographical account of deafness.

He also edited *Longer Contemporary Poems* (1966), the *Penguin Book of English Romantic Verse* (1968) and the *Penguin Book of Everyday Verse* (1976). His own published poetry included *Moral Stories* (1954), *Monologue of a Deaf Man* (1958), *Adam at Evening* (1965), *To the gods the Shades: New and Collected Poems* (1981); *Selected Poems* (1988) and *Elegies* (1990).

Wright's poetry has a unique conversational yet thoughtful and original tone and content: in general, it is not dissimilar in style to Nicholson's own work.

In 1951, Wright married the New Zealand actress, Philippa ("Pippa") Reid (d. 1985). Pippa joined the cast of the Century Theatre ('Blue Box') and in 1967 they moved to live in Braithwaite, on the outskirts of Keswick in Cumberland.

It was around this time that Nicholson first made contact, originally with Pippa, probably having heard of the relocation from their mutual poet friend, John Heath-Stubbs. Norman and Yvonne subsequently became close friends with the Wrights and they became regular correspondents and frequent visitors to each other's homes. Prior to this, Nicholson wrote in a letter[140] to his friend Daniel Hay at Whitehaven that the profoundly deaf poet David Wright had relocated to Braithwaite, and that by all accounts his wife Philippa should make quite a considerable impact upon the local community - maybe just a bit of male to male innuendo, but Nicholson was to become a close friend of both Pippa and David Wright.

This period of friendship took in the deaths both of Yvonne Nicholson from cancer, in 1982, and of Pippa Wright from a brain tumour in 1985, and the preserved correspondence poignantly records these shattering events in the lives of the two poets.

Following Yvonne Nicholson's death, her friend Peggy Troll was able to provide Norman with car transport beyond Millom. In 1984, for Nicholson's seventieth birthday *Festschrift, Between Comets,* Wright compiled a colloquial yet deeply insightful tribute poem, which traced the route from Braithwaite to Millom, past all the industrial dereliction and pollution of the West Cumbrian coastal strip until:

And then there's Ravenglass, and the bird-haunted
Sand-dunes lagooning a derelict sea.
This, Norman is your country and your home,
And where your verse lives rooted like a tree
To where it grows, feeding its leaves therefrom.[141]

Wright was re-married, to the wife of his late lifelong friend, Oonagh Swift, in 1987. Wright died from cancer in Waldron. East Sussex, in August 1994.

4

Literary Apprenticeship, 1932-1937

Nicholson's return to Millom from Linford TB Sanatorium for researchers might be compared figuratively to embarkation on a voyage into previously uncharted waters. His continued regular correspondence with Sylvia Lubelsky is a significant and useful aid to navigation in this regard. In addition, and as has already been mentioned, much later in his life, Nicholson was interviewed in depth by the local BBC Radio Station, in part discussing (but not too frankly) events in his life after Linford

Gardner in his thesis describes Nicholson's stunned feelings in 1932 upon being jolted from clean and rural Linford back into the midst of dirty industrial Millom. Nicholson himself much later wrote that he had been appalled by the lack of fresh and pure air in Millom and by the severe industrial pollution everywhere: this comment was made notably in a 1964 BBC book, *Writers on Themselves.*[142] He recalled in some detail the circumstances of his return to Millom in 1932, perceiving this grime-laden urban environment as totally alien to the healthy, sylvan countryside which he had previously inhabited. After Linford, Nicholson complied in every detail with his sanatorium doctors' orders, taking twice-daily country walks, almost whatever the weather. The reactions of the Millom townsfolk upon encountering this singularly-attired, 'posh'-speaking 'returned native'[143] must have been of some astonishment!

Norman's letters to Sylvia often recount his striving to master the craft of poetry, as well as describing summer evenings spent in enjoyment of the company of the 'damsels' at the nearby cricket field. In his much later local radio interviews, he laboured at some length his point that most aspiring writers try for several years to get published, then nearly all give up in the face of universal rejections, and move on to an alternative and far more secure way of earning a living. But he had had no such option, he explained, and had therefore been compelled to persevere with his writing for over a decade, until eventually becoming established as a paid author. The deep and painful physical rift which Nicholson had experienced upon returning home developed into a spiritual one too, which (fortunately for him) slowly repaired itself in his mind. This possibly marks the beginning of Nicholson adopting his perspective upon the natural world and the whole of life as an inevitable, integrated, cyclical and living whole, encompassing even the slag banks and ore mines of Millom within its interdependent unity.

Nicholson felt that he had been almost miraculously granted a second chance of remaining alive. He often associated himself with the widow's son, in the story of Elijah; this motif was, a decade or so later, to resurface in Nicholson's successful verse play, *The Old Man of the Mountains*.

Regaining his religious faith was integral to this bridging or healing process within Nicholson, and out of all this fertile ground grew up creative shoots which would blossom as his verse drama and the themes of much of his early poetry. A devout Anglican communicant in his early teens, Nicholson had, like many of his generation, embraced socialism and rejected religion in response to the economic slump and political climate of the early 1930s. By 1933 he was still entirely agnostic: for example, in that year and his Christmas letter to Sylvia he referred, rather vehemently, to the Christmas festival as the needless celebration of a birth that had led to two thousand years of self-deception, hypocrisy and humbug. Nicholson's contemporaries had of course taken the route out of Millom that his own health had denied to him, of going up to university. For just one example, Bessie Satterthwaite in 1933 had gone to Manchester University to read English. Bessie soon joined the Student Christian Movement there, and participated enthusiastically in their annual national conferences.

The significance of the encounter with T.S. Eliot's early poetry and its momentous and absolutely intoxicating effect on Nicholson has already been mentioned, but was so influential as regards his development as a poet that it is deliberately repeated here, in the context of this Chapter. In the summer of 1934 in Millom cricket field he first read Eliot's early poetry, including *The Waste Land*. He much later described how for months thereafter he had lived constantly under the influence of *The Waste Land*, and had sought out and devoured all of Eliot's quoted sources, such as Frazer's *Golden Bough*; he recalled, too, that he had once stopped and clutched another friend in the street, to ask if he had yet read *'the greatest poem in the English language.'*[144]

From this point on, Nicholson resolved to tread in Eliot's footsteps by becoming a poet and writer himself. It required of Nicholson many years of hard labour before he developed his own poetic voice and achieved any significant published success, but his letters to Sylvia reveal that, as early as in 1935, he had begun work on a novel with *'some good writing amongst it'* and on a short story.

Nicholson once declared later in his life that encountering the work of TS Eliot had resulted in his return to religious belief.[145] Far from debunking Christianity, it had seemed to Nicholson that Eliot's quoted sources such as Frazer's *Golden Bough* pointed the way towards compelling reasons to <u>believe</u> in Christianity, and Nicholson's personal religious faith as a result was reawakened and was affirmed by him throughout the remainder of his life. He seems to have moved towards a theological outlook similar to that of Charles Williams's *Way of the Affirmation of Images*. For example, Nicholson perceived in each and all the basic cycles of nature, that death was entirely natural and integral: a very necessary prerequisite for the continuance of all life. He cited Matthew, 10:39:

> *He that findeth his life shall lose it; and he that loseth his life shall find it.*

5

Early Works, 1937-1947

This entire era was one of drastic change in almost all aspects of national life, everything moving ultimately to a war footing. There was a resurgence of popular interest in all things generally spiritual and specifically religious, particularly Christian, which inevitably raised ethical, social and political debates about that nebulous 'better future' for which everyone was so ardently fighting: that place 'somewhere over the rainbow'.

This prevailing climate inevitably influenced Norman Nicholson's early works. For example, in 1941, Bishop Temple's Malvern Conference in an extraordinary act of faith determined an ambitious agenda for post-war reconstruction along Christian and egalitarian principles. Many individual writers and thinkers whose names constantly recur within these pages, such as George Every, S.L. Bethell, Michael Roberts and Charles Williams poured their individual and collective thoughts into this early iteration of a 'think tank'.

But, to return to Nicholsonian specifics: in July 1937[146], Bessie Satterthwaite attended the conference of the Student Christian Movement at Swanwick in Derbyshire. Here George Every was lecturing to delegates about modern poetry. Bessie mentioned her poet-friend Nicholson to Every, and showed Every some examples of his work. Every was impressed, and asked Bessie for Nicholson's address. The outcome was that Every sent the samples to T.S. Eliot for his appraisal and comment, and to his friend the poet Michael Roberts. Eliot's response, although characteristically cautious, was one of (for him) considerable enthusiasm, whilst Roberts was sufficiently impressed to write Nicholson a long letter of encouragement, along with assorted technical tips and advice, including that he might, using Roberts' recommendation, submit some of his poetry to the American periodical *Poetry (Chicago).*

In late December, 1937, Nicholson did as previously advised, submitting a poem he titled *Song for 7 pm*, which was accepted by the then *Poetry (Chicago)* Editor, the American poet, George Dillon, who included it in a 1938 issue[147] and went on to invite further submissions from Nicholson. These emerged as a pair of poems, *Poem in Pencil* and *Poem in Ink* (sent in April, 1938), but they were never published. *Sonnet for an Introvert* was, however, published in January, 1939.[148] But none of these poems have appeared in Neil Curry's (Ed.), *Norman Nicholson: Collected Poems.*

As at the year 1937, not one national UK publisher had accepted any of Nicholson's poetry, although two poems had been published during 1937 in *The Serpent,* a Manchester University student-published literary magazine. Bessie Satterthwaite may possibly have facilitated this.

And no data survives which might explain the circumstances of the publication of a few early Nicholson poems in a 1938 Oxford University student literary magazine titled *Bolero*, which emanated from Worcester College and was edited by budding-poet John (later, Sir John) Waller[149]. This magazine was the forerunner of the longer surviving and better known literary journal, *Kingdom Come*[150], to which Nicholson was also to become a regular contributor. *Bolero's* editorials very much reflect the preoccupation with the need for literature to reflect modern urban life, as opposed to the Romantic and the Picturesque. Travel Agents then advertised within *Bolero's* pages fourteen-day package holidays to Venice for a price of around £12, whilst a rather sinister-looking organisation calling itself 'Friends of National Spain' appealed for sympathisers to make a donation to their campaign to help the Fascists there to 'preserve European civilisation and culture'.

The following 1938 *Bolero* editorial by Waller is typical both of the feelings of the age in general and of some of Nicholson's own key beliefs which were sometimes articulated in Nicholson's topographical prose: for example via his exhortations that Cumbria should be treated as a working, changing region and not simply the scenic parts alone selected and venerated and generally regarded as immutable or preserved in aspic:

The goal of modern poetry has not yet been generally achieved. In the last twenty years the changes made in form and technique have been colossal, but, carried away perhaps by these same changes, poets have neglected what should be their primary function. This is the accurate study of men and women and the world seen in relation to men and women.

Without some such function I am not sure that the technical changes are of any importance. There is no merit in the use of modern diction and advanced vers libre if one is to use them, as Mr Grigson might put it, to shoot right up the airy mountain.

The poet of to-day, if he is to be of any future significance, must come down to earth. Present day scenery is made up of factory chimneys, slums, cinema houses, advertisement hoardings, and dance halls.

It is a world in which people work in mines, are a cog in the machinery of mass-production, take a holiday to watch football, go to the seaside for a week-end, and snatch the greater part of their education from the newspapers. These are facts that the poet must recognize. Green fields and country lanes are the delight of a comparative few.

But even if this were not the case man with his labours and pleasures is far more urgent than the landscape or the philosophic imagery. Living poetry needs to be about

> *people, and the word people must comprise all. The poet must study not merely Peter who plays rugby, but Paul who runs about in the gutter, not merely Lady Casanova but Jane the barmaid of "The Golden Farmer"; not merely Rudolph the artist but Edward Bastaple the maker of automobiles.*
>
> *Mass Observation*[151] *is a science and is therefore not primarily a literary concern, but its broader principles all writers might do well to adopt. "Look in thy heart and write," said Sidney when he desired to pen love sonnets to Stella. Nowadays it should be a case of "Look around you and write".*
>
> *The 20th century is an interesting age and those who can paint it vividly will be read at a future date.*

Nicholson's *Poem on Thursday* appeared in *Bolero* Issue One, and two poems by him, *Behead a God* and *Beside a War Memorial* in the second Issue. None of these have survived into the *Collected Poems*.

Nicholson's *Bolero* poems appeared alongside others by the eighteen-year-old Keith Douglas, with whom Nicholson in 1943, had a selection of his poems published, along with some by Douglas's contemporary at Oxford, J.C. Hall (1920-2011). Douglas's poetic career was cut short, tragically, when he was killed in action in Normandy in 1944. (Douglas's mother subsequently made Hall her late son's literary executor).[152]

A little earlier, in 1941, Nicholson, having in 1940 returned to the Anglican Church as a full communicant, had persuaded Penguin Books to commission him to edit a proposed *Penguin Anthology of Religious Verse*, for which Penguin paid him an advance of £100.[153] This was duly published, in 1942, and, consistent with the wartime religious resurgence, sold a very respectable 30,000 copies. But nonetheless it brought scant monetary reward to Nicholson. After having to buy personally and in advance of publication all the necessary copyright permissions, his net profit from the book amounted to just seven pounds.[154]

However, from a reputational standpoint, the book must have been hugely significant to the 28-year-old Nicholson. Bravely, he had chosen broadly and widely from the work of contemporary poets, some of whom not been hitherto classified as conventionally 'religious', such as Auden, Yeats, D.H. Lawrence and Dylan Thomas. The Editor of *The Church Times* much approved:

> *...Mr Nicholson has done his work exceedingly well, for this is a volume which can fitly be placed beside Lord David Cecil's most satisfactory anthology of Christian poetry...*[155]

Nicholson, having acquired a literary reputation was beginning regularly to have poems and articles published in periodicals such as *New English Weekly, The Listener* and *New Statesman and Nation*.

Also, in 1943, Nicholson published his literary survey, *Man and Literature*, (SCM Press), which he had based largely upon his work between 1938 and 1943 as an evening-class Tutor for the Workers' Educational Association, at first in Millom[156], then later, further afield, in various West Cumberland towns and villages, such as in Whitehaven[157] and St. Bees. Mill Hill (Public) School had been evacuated from North London to the St. Bees Public School campus, so Nicholson found there a very different audience for his lectures than the predominantly working class West Cumbrians.

Nicholson in 1939, had lectured at the Student Christian Movement Conference on the topic of 'Morals and the Modern Novel'[158]. This material, too, formed the basis for the fuller *Man and Literature* book.[159]

His first impressions of the rather grim, very deprived colliery and iron ore mining towns of the West Cumbrian Coastal Plain between the mountains and the sea came as something quite startling to Nicholson. In a 1980s local radio interview, he recalled having been deeply affected by his visits to these towns and villages, in particular by the ordinary inhabitants' constant battle with grinding poverty, and Nicholson mentioned to his interviewer that these places had evoked in him echoes of the old Border ballads which had greatly influenced his early poetry.[160]

Eliot, at Faber and Faber, possibly lobbied by his trusted assistant and Nicholson's friend and ally Anne Ridler, published Norman's first full, solo, poetry collection, *Five Rivers*, in 1944.[161] The very fine, fresh and original, title poem, along with many others, were inspired by the sights and impressions of Nicholson's coastal train journeys along that spectacular railway line[162] from Millom to Whitehaven, alongside the estuaries of five West Cumbrian rivers and their disparate environs as the rivers each flow into the ubiquitous Irish Sea to the west: these are the rivers Esk, Mite, Irt, Calder and Ehen. Some other poems in the collection, such as the ambitious *Bow in the Cloud*, are not overtly topographical, but are wholly or predominantly, religious in theme; the latter poem rather startlingly transposes the Biblical events of Noah and The Great Flood into Nicholson's familiar Cumberland fells. This kind of transposition appeared again, in Nicholson's (1948) rather successful first verse play, *The Old Man of the Mountains*.

Generally, an entirely enthusiastic and favourable reception was given to the first publication of *Five Rivers*. It gained Nicholson the Royal Society of Literature's inaugural Heinemann Award in 1945 and Nicholson was at about the same time acclaimed by his literary peers when elected to a Fellowship of the same Royal Society (F.R.S.L.). The book, even by 1945, had gone through two reprints, and it firmly cemented the foundations of Nicholson's forthcoming lifelong relationship with Faber and Faber.

Nicholson had previously submitted the collection to *Poetry (London)* but that contemporary literary luminary, its editor, Tambimuttu (1915-1983) had rejected it. Nicholson was perhaps fortunate to have had Anne Ridler on hand in order to put it in front of T.S. Eliot himself: nonetheless, Eliot ultimately judged himself it to merit the prestigious Faber imprint.[163]

6

Middle and Later Years

This, perhaps the most settled part of Nicholson's life, is not in any great detail recounted here: the various other chapters of this book already adequately tell of significant events in both his literary and domestic life, each in their particular context: it is felt that merely collating them separately and out of context would add little of value to this study.

Nearly everyone's lives tend to be touched by parental deaths, and most by at least one marriage or similar life-changing events concerning close family members. In Nicholson's case, his father, Joseph, died in 1954, aged seventy-seven, leaving Norman as a reluctant Gentleman's Outfitter Shop proprietor for two months, until he found a tenant for the shop premises.[164]

Nicholson's stepmother, Rosetta, remained, alongside Norman, resident of 14 St. George's Terrace until her own death fifteen years later, in 1969, at the age of eighty-two. Norman had married in 1956, so for thirteen years he was looked after by two women. He always referred to Rosetta as 'mother' and treated her family as if they were that of his natural mother.

Freelance journalism and assorted published prose as well as a succession of plays occupied Nicholson's life and works during his middle years; his 1954 poetry collection *The Pot Geranium* was to become the last one he was to publish during a period of eighteen years, until 1972. During the same period, contemporaries such as Philip Larkin and Ted Hughes were consolidating their reputations as leading English poets, but Nicholson was curiously silent, at least as regards any published collections of new poetry. Public readings of his past poetry, along with school visits formed a big part of Nicholson's life during this period. He and Yvonne visited many and miscellaneous locations throughout the local area and sometimes beyond.

Nicholson's fallow period, as regards published poetry was more than a glitch: it was a serious hiatus, which is further discussed later[165], but it is perhaps worth speculating here whether changes to Nicholson's domestic life and circumstances may have exerted any significant influence.

Nicholson's early poetry had been the outcome of various highly-intense and overwhelming emotions welling-up within him and bursting out in the form of poetry. For example: his discovery of Eliot; his adoption of a strong personal religious faith; his first serious love for another person. He had as a result entered a state of intense excitement which had acted as the necessary catalyst for his first 'good' poetry.[166] One might speculate that by the time of his marriage to Yvonne, this fervour had largely dissipated and Nicholson had in a sense fallen into something of a comfortable but creatively-toxic domestic rut, being by then moderately successful as a writer and looked after very comprehensively and rather comfortably by not one, but two women.

In a local newspaper interview, Nicholson himself gave the following explanation:

> *...I stopped writing partly because 1 had ceased to be fashionable with the coming of people like Philip Larkin but also because I had finished a particular phase of my work. The reason I started again was because of the influence of my wife. Her contribution was enormous to my more-recent work. I started to write about people. I became much more concerned with inter-relationships which wasn't something which had interested me before. I began writing about the people of Millom, starting with my uncles. I realised that if I didn't write about the town and the people then, it would be too late, for Millom was in decline. At the same time I'm still interested in the pure elements of the landscape...*[167]

This explanation only partially tallies with others given by Nicholson, in particular with a published interview with his friend, the poet David Wright. Nicholson's poetry simply falling out of fashion is indeed a common theme, but Nicholson encountering Robert Lowell's *Life Studies*, first published in 1959, is this time cited as the other key factor: he makes no mention of his wife's influence in the matter.[168] Similarly, interviewed during the 1970s by the local BBC radio station, Nicholson attributed his poetic renaissance to Lowell's influence, despite (Nicholson hastened to add) their respective poetic styles being *'miles apart'*.

Nicholson once, in this context deployed the mining image of having worked his seam out. This concept does seem to resemble aspects of T.S. Eliot's literary theory, in particular Eliot's *Tradition and the Individual Talent*[169] in which Eliot postulated that an individual poet isolated from literary tradition would sooner or later run out of creative steam. Extending the commonality with Eliot in a very different but perhaps still relevant direction, both Eliot and Nicholson achieved great happiness as a result of loving marriages made somewhat serendipitously rather late in their respective lives. It is perhaps understandable given Nicholson's (and indeed perhaps Eliot's) life circumstances that his former rather ascetic outlook changed to a far more humanist one, and that this change resulted from his marriage.

In a local radio interview, Nicholson did once mention Yvonne's effective care for him as having restored his physical health and stamina sufficiently to enable him to start writing poetry again, but this hardly in itself adequately explains the long interruption in the poetry alone, whilst his outputs of prose and verse plays continued unabated.

Nicholson had been married for just three years when Robert Lowell's *Life Studies* was first published in Britain.

If reading this book had really restarted him writing poetry, then it is indicative of his very very lengthy poetic gestation periods that the next collection was not ready until some twelve years later.

In Eliotic style, Nicholson borrowed the title of his eventual (1973) collection, *A Local Habitation* from literary heritage – from Shakespeare's A *Midsummer Night's Dream* (4.1):

> *The poet's eye, in a fine frenzy rolling,*
> *Doth glance from heaven to earth, from earth to heaven;*
> *And as imagination bodies forth*
> *The forms of things unknown, the poet's pen*
> *Turns them to shapes, and gives to airy nothing*
> *A local habitation and a name.*

Despite its shift in subject matter, this shift in the focus of Nicholson's poetry remained rather curiously distant in its approach, in that Nicholson wrote descriptively about his family members but hardly ever about anyone's - particularly his own – inner life: he continued to shy-away from 'introspection', perhaps.

7

Nicholson at Seventy

Nicholson reached the age of seventy in 1984. By then he was living quietly and alone at 14 St. George's Terrace as a widower, his wife, Yvonne, having died in 1982. His last volume of poetry, *Sea to the West* had been published in the same year. Norman was now largely confined to places within walking distance having never learned to drive, and having formerly relied upon Yvonne for transport anywhere beyond Millom.

1984 was to become a most eventful year for Nicholson.

Bustling television and film crews descended upon Norman in particular and upon Millom in general to compile a feature for London Weekend Television's South Bank Show, edited and introduced by Melvyn Bragg, (himself a fellow Cumbrian). The Director was John Read (1923-2011), an accomplished, former BBC documentary maker, who in the past had directed at-length film studies of many prominent subjects, including L.S. Lowry, Henry Moore and Barbara Hepworth.

Nicholson's late wife's sister's daughter, Elizabeth Joyce, had been married in April, 1984. To celebrate the occasion, Nicholson, despite having written very little poetry since 1980, produced one of his most accomplished later poems, *Epithalamium for a Niece.*

At Millom town library, in July, 1984, a bronze head[170] likeness of Nicholson by the sculptress Joan Palmer was unveiled[171]. Nicholson politely ridiculed those who called this 'his bust', but responded with a very gracious acceptance speech at the actual ceremony. A contemporary press report mentions that he was 'visibly moved'[172]. He also warmly thanked all those who had helped him following the death of his wife.

Joan Palmer, the head's sculptress, had been evacuated to Millom during the War, and had donated all her considerable time and skill, only charging for the materials involved and the transport costs etc. Even so, the total cost had been £525 - a not inconsiderable sum thirty years ago.

One might speculate about how well the evacuee, the young Joan Palmer, had known the young Norman Nicholson, back then, in order to grow to so admire and ultimately to honour him so very much, but there are no surviving records or memories to shed any more light on the matter.

It was indicative of Millom Town Council's rather polarised and, on the part of a minority of councillors, downright jaundiced views about Nicholson and his worth to the town, that the Council had only been willing to pay for its wooden stand and for a few incidentals, leaving it to all other donors to fund the bulk of the overall charges. Some councillors had nonetheless objected to the Council having to insure this valuable work of art which it had been given virtually for free!

In September, accompanied by much pomp and ceremony in Whitehaven, Norman was made the very first honorary Freeman of his native Borough of Copeland.

And, during 1984, came the award of an honorary D.Litt. from Lancaster University, a 'bar' to his existing (1980) honorary doctorate from Liverpool University.

A further notable event during 1984 was the publication of *Between Comets: for Norman Nicholson at 70,* a Festschrift compilation book for Nicholson, from fellow poets and prominent literary figures of the day. It was edited by the Cockermouth poet, William Scammell, and included poetry and prose tributes from Seamus Heaney, Ted Hughes, R.S. Thomas, Charles Causley, Melvyn Bragg, and many others.

It was published by the (now defunct) Taxvs (sic) Press at Durham, in a first and only edition of just 700 copies. It was a small paperback, with a distinctive front cover illustration by Ian R. Steel along with a frontispiece sketch of Norman in his Millom Town habitat, drawn by Chris Barnfather. A further 50 copies of the book were bound specially in cloth hard covers, into a numbered, limited edition signed both by Scammell and by Nicholson. A further bound presentation copy was reserved for Nicholson himself.

Nicholson presented his great friend, George Every, with

a copy of this book as a 1984 Christmas present, warmly inscribed thus, in his usual barely-legible handwriting[173] :

> *George -with all Christmas Greetings (looks like (love?) the humble subject of this Book.*

Between Comets stands as testimony to the very high esteem in which Nicholson was held by his peers in the literary community. Editor William Scammell's brief Introduction, exuded the deepest admiration:

> *For fifty years (he) has pursued his vocation, which is a lonely and difficult one, with the greatest distinction. We offer him this tribute in honour of his life and work.*

And, in a stirring conclusion, Scammell wrote:

> *Thanks to him (Nicholson) we know it (Millom and environs) as well as we know Eastwood, Haworth and Bockhampton. Though he couldn't say Boo to a goose[174] and was packed off to dry dock[175] for early repair, he has gone on a splendid voyage, and spoken for us all.*

This compact book affords, on almost every turn of its, sixty-odd pages, a multiplicity of acute and expert perspectives on Nicholson's work, in both poem and prose essay form.

For example, Seamus Heaney chose rather magnificently to contribute thus to *Between Comets*:

A Paved Text
For Norman Nicholson

Dialect landlocked
in a maritime district,
stone walls in earshot
of rowlocks and the seawrack –

those Cumbrian phonetics
cracked like a plaited whip
until the slack, nostalgic rambler in me trotted

on the paved margin
of my own black pool…

Heaney, later as part of this significant contribution, goes on to endorse and to echo in bitter and doom-laden terms, Nicholson's own unease about the potential environmental perils from the West Cumbrian Windscale[176] (Sellafield) nuclear facility, e.g.:

Now nuclear poisons / re-anglicize a sea....

Unlike some other contributors, Heaney seems to have taken the trouble to write a bespoke tribute poem, as opposed to simply 'recycling' a stock one, written earlier.

Other poems included tributes by Neil Curry[177], Charles Causley, Anne Ridler and many more.

Melvyn Bragg, who had once himself accompanied Nicholson in a public reading, described Nicholson in an essay within the same book, as:

...the finest Cumbrian born since Wordsworth, the undisputed laureate of the Lakes.

8

The Novels

Nicholson is, of course, best known for his poetry, but his poetry in a way is just the distillation of his much more dilute literary outpourings, from book reviewing and broadcasting, topographical guidebook writing, making carol / song lyrics, stage playwriting, and even two published, full length novels.

This Chapter focuses on these novels, which date from the mid-1940s, when Norman Nicholson was a youngish man of around thirty. *The Fire of the Lord* was the first to be published, in 1944, followed by *The Green Shore*, in 1947.[178]

Now long ago out of print and largely overlooked if not forgotten, even by academics and Norman Nicholson enthusiasts, these novels seem to have glimmered only fleetingly in the world of published fiction and then quickly faded away.

Even Norman himself seems to have virtually disowned them in later life. During a 1970s local radio interview, he claimed that he could not even remember their titles.

Although in one sense they are now relics, these Nicholson novels are still in many ways well worth seeking out and reading. Although both are 'kitchen sink' close-ups of the daily lives and experiences of small-town (fictional) characters as opposed to anything grander or more wide-ranging in scope, they are nonetheless reasonably engaging and interesting stories. In addition, at least in parts they represent hugely interesting - albeit thinly disguised - portraits of Norman Nicholson as a younger man, and, as such, expose some of the foundations which underpin both the plays and the poems.

Preceding Nicholson's published novels there had been one published short story, titled *Pisgah*[179], along with several unpublished attempts at novels. *Pisgah* has obvious autobiographical components, the central character called Sam having been bedridden for six years as a result of an underground mining accident. The ironworks transmutes in the story to a new chemical factory under construction, the giant chimney of which becomes visible in Sam's bedroom window. Sam develops a richly fertile imagination as a result of this physical and social isolation; he also feels much guilt that he has turned out to be a financial millstone around the neck of his parents.[180]

Gardner, in his thesis (p. 128) mentions some of the probable influences upon one of Nicholson's unpublished novels titled *Love to the Nth* as having been the novels of Ivy Compton Burnett,[181] Virginia Woolf and James Joyce.

Another unpublished novel was possibly an attempt by Nicholson to write a novel to a formula which would make it a bestseller. He gave this novel the bizarre title of *The Cat's got the Toothache*, and evidently had high hopes for its future success, but these were dashed totally by Eliot's rejection of it, accompanied by some quite severe criticism[182].

This particular rejection may have led to a significant turning point in the whole of Nicholson's literary development. Gardner's thesis reports, at p. 132, that Nicholson wrote, in a letter to George Every in March of 1940 that he was seeking to eradicate the 'introspective' aspects of his work, in view of Eliot's low opinion of his efforts

A distinct reluctance to use introspection is certainly often evident across the whole range of Nicholson's work. Similarly, more than thirty years after writing that letter to Every, Nicholson declared to a local BBC radio interviewer that he normally wouldn't consider events in his own personal life as being at all suitable themes for exposition in his poetry.

Turning to the two published novels, they are broadly similar in that the principal characters of both are young working-class inhabitants of the small coastal industrial town of Odborough - very obviously representing the real town of Millom.

The two novels are very similar too in theme and technique, as well as in style. Both of them have allegorical or symbolical Christian themes, the earlier one Biblical, this concerning the cleansing, fertility-restoring nature of Pentecostal Fire as well as the story of Elijah's sacrifice, at 1 Kings 18, verse 38._Similarly, *The Green Shore* uses as its epigraph an extract from William Morris poem, *A Garden by the Sea,* specifically:

> *Dark shore no ship has ever seen,*
> *Tormented by the billows green*
> *Whose murmur comes unceasingly*
> *Unto the place for which I cry.*
> *For which I cry both day and night,*
> *For which I let slip all delight,*
> *That maketh me both deaf and blind,*
> *Careless to win, unskilled to find*
> *And quick to lose what all men seek.*

The two novels both focus upon the lives and loves and spiritual journeys of certain young adult inhabitants of the town of Odborough/(clearly, Millom); the novels each recount vividly the life of ordinary young people within a small and close-knit industrial community, when unconventional intellectual and spiritual interlopers enter their lives and challenge their established beliefs and attitudes.

And, quite unlike Nicholson's poetry or plays, both of these novels positively throb with passion.

Nicholson's fictional male and female characters are attracted like magnets; those so attracted indulge in sensual, bodily touching – rather tame, perhaps, to contemporary tastes, yet nonetheless intended to be vicariously electrifying and thrilling to 1940s readers – touchings, usually of elbows and forearms or other ordinarily innocuous bodily appendages, but sometimes in moments of exceptional intensity going so far as to involve the groping of bosoms - all very sexy content indeed, for that era.

These carnal urges inevitably clash with the protagonists' religious faith and moral principles - a challenging scenario, indeed, and one which the young Nicholson must have experienced personally, and, probably, acutely.

The Fire of the Lord is generally less overtly raunchy than the second novel, but is otherwise similar. It anticipated by a decade or so the small-town goings-on of the American bestseller, *Peyton Place*. It focuses on two interlocking love triangles: one involves Maggie Birker, a comely middle-aged businesswoman, who runs a successful small bakery from her home, supplying bread and pies and cakes to the townsfolk. Maggie was married when young to a much older man, Benjamin Fell, who not long afterwards experienced a conversion into something of a nonconformist religious zealot and walked out on his young wife in order to adopt the life of an itinerant preacher. After many years of absence Benjy was eventually presumed dead, and Maggie married the much younger Jim Birker, a skilled patternmaker[183] by trade, who is employed in the nearby industrial centre of 'Furness' (obviously the fictionalised nearby town of Barrow-in-Furness). Maggie has Jim very firmly under her thumb, whilst Jim responds by immersing himself completely in his (shift) work; he and Maggie live together under the same roof, but otherwise seem to lead entirely separate emotional existences.

Maggie employs a young, deaf girl, Elsie Holliwell, a devout Anglican churchgoer. Elsie and Jim move from a relationship of mutual indifference to one of intimacy and passion, as a result both of Maggie's loveless subjugation of Jim and through their natural affinity simply as two young people who are thrown frequently together.

Meanwhile, Maggie's first husband, Benjy, has returned to his native town, and to the farm where he was brought up, which had since been bought by the Odborough Ironworks Company, in order to tip molten blast furnace slag into arid hills all over its surrounding land. Benjy's family farmhouse has fallen into dereliction, but he clandestinely moves himself into it, and makes a nuisance of himself with the town policeman (a bumbling character who is the comic relief of the book but who also lusts after Maggie), the particular nuisance arising from Benjy's obsession with raising all manner of fires during a time when strict wartime blackout rules were in force.

The arrival of 'Old Benjy' is glossed-over by Maggie as merely the visit of the deranged uncle of her first husband, and Benjy seems to go along with this subterfuge. But Benjy constantly proclaims that 'the fire of the Lord' must consume and purify all the useless and unclean man-made and natural dross, before new life and fertility can ever begin to grow. This 'Green' theme, relating in particular to responsible land use and the perils of greedy, intensive farming practices, might be seen as a significant precursor to Norman Nicholson's later works, particularly his successful verse play, *The Old Man of the Mountains.*

The novel's physical setting involves darkness, of course in a sense the antithesis of Fire. This is the darkness both of the strict wartime blackout and of dark winter months of the year. The characters strive each in their own way to find a way through their personal darkness, into the spiritual light symbolised by the Fire of the Lord.

Elsie and Jim ultimately become lovers, but not without much soul-searching on Elsie's part, whilst Benjy - appropriately and symbolically - meets his end cremated by the lethally hot and fiery ironworks' slag whilst it is being tipped over his ancestral farmlands.

Benjy's death has many repercussions. Jim's marriage to Maggie was not lawful or valid, given that Benjy had been still alive when it took place, so Jim and Elsie become free to pursue their lives together. The book closes with Jim suggesting that they start a new life together '*somewhere where nobody knows us*'. A densely descriptive and lyrical passage then follows, packed with vivid images of Nature and the earth's fertility and the fulfilling nature of community bonds and life and even of the Resurrection. Elsie, contemplating all this intensity of feeling, firmly declines to abandon her roots.

Elsie's fictionalized thoughts perhaps closely mirror Nicholson's personal reasons as to why he himself resolved never to leave Millom: they possibly stand for his own reasons for valuing 'belonging' to a small, close-knit town community and being a part of God's universal processes. Later, in a BBC Home Service *Lift up Your Hearts* broadcast, he expanded with his usual penetrating and lucid imagery along similar lines:

> *The universe is not just a huge mechanical coffee-grinder, ticking over and over without aim or purpose. It works to a pattern; it works to a plan. And part of the sheer enjoyment of being among mountains comes from our sometimes feeling swept up in the plan, where every end is a new beginning and every death a new birth*[184].

The Green Shore similarly features a young, rather sensitive, disabled central character (this time with a leg iron), in the form of Alice Dale, as well as another strange, older, prophetic figure who has chosen for religious reasons to shun conventional society, this time named Anthony Pengwilly ('Old Pen') who inhabits an isolated cottage near a former lighthouse on the outskirts of the town. Anthony, in this verdant and light-suffused environment, replaces and contrasts with the Old Benjy of the earlier novel, holed-up in his dark, desolate slag bank farmhouse. Anthony's monkish, hermit-like ways of living and feeling collide head-on with his swelling affection for Alice, and Alice herself has to reconcile her own heartfelt religious and spiritual principles and her conventional small-town morality with her stirring and compelling passion for this much older man.

Concurrently, another love story is working its way out, in the matter of Alice's relationship with a boy of her own age, namely, Alan Grizebeck, who eventually makes a clumsy pass at her whilst crammed beside her in the back of a motor van during an excursion to 'Blackport' Music

Festival (obviously, this is the coal port of Whitehaven, up the coast). There is passing mention too, as regards this excursion, of 'Burnet Scales', clearly in reality the little West Cumbrian Victorian seaside resort of Seascale.

There exists a very tenuous but intriguing possible link between the plot of *Fire of the Lord* and Nicholson's actual personal life. It is known that, certainly around 1950, he was very friendly with a Millom girl who was twelve years his junior[185].

This real life event may possibly have happened a little later than c. 1946, when the novel was probably written, but, equally possibly, one might speculate that this same relationship may well have started or have been in progress during the gestation of this novel.

Just after the end of the War, Nicholson had ended his close relationship with Enrica Garnier[186]. It is known that Nicholson's romance with the young Millom woman ended in c.1951. In fact, by 1952, this woman had married a man from nearby Barrow in Furness, where she worked as a school teacher.

Prof. Philip Gardner has reported that Nicholson had originally intended to call *The Green Shore* (for obvious reasons) *No Man is an Island,* but the title had been used already, for another, unconnected, book.

Critical appraisal of Nicholson's novels cannot realistically claim them to be works of notable quality or any particular accomplishment. They are indeed rather flawed, and in parts they are heavy-handedly over-written. But neither arguably do they at all merit their present, almost complete, oblivion, nor do they deserve the dismissive, very low esteem in which Nicholson himself seems to have regarded them. On the contrary, they do offer many valuable insights into Nicholson's future personal and literary development; they are, in their own right, reasonably well-plotted and, in parts, quite well-written sagas of small town life, which a present-day script or screenplay writer could perhaps readily turn into a rather gripping modern drama.

Thus, *The Fire of the Lord* for instance contains much that is in reality Millom and surrounding area and its characters represent some of the town's real-life inhabitants, barely-fictionalised. The plot, too, mirrors numerous actual events in the life of Nicholson and of his family. For example, in the book, Pengwilly's mother had, exactly like Nicholson's grandmother, crossed the Duddon Sands by carrier's cart in order to settle in the burgeoning new town of Millom, and had been so horrified by her first glimpse of the place that she had asked the carter to turn around and to convey her back. And, to cite just a few of many: the fictional Anthony Pengwilly, like Nicholson's father, had been apprenticed to one of the town's tailors and outfitters; Nicholson's grandmother, like Anthony's mother, had been severely disabled, following a fall; Nicholson's stepmother, just like the Pengwillys, was of West Country tin mining stock; Nicholson, like Anthony Pengwilly, had been immersed in Nonconformist Chapel life, and Anthony's mother, as Nicholson's too, had died as a result of the 1918/19 influenza pandemic.

Characters such as many of the town's shopkeepers and trades-people along with particular members of the Chapel Choir migrated from these novels, to reappear in Nicholson's later prose, both in *Provincial Pleasures* and in his later autobiography, *Wednesday Early Closing.*[187]

Similarly, in *The Green Shore*, Odborough / Millom and its environment, both natural and built, features so massively as to risk becoming repetitious and overdone. The character of Anthony Pengwilly is clearly modelled upon the hermit, ascetic, life of St. Anthony, and both this character, along with his interactions with his young friend Alice, represent very early examples of Nicholson's interest in the theological ideas of Charles Williams.

The mature Pengwilly, the recluse and aesthete and his first encounter with the much younger Alice Dale, is the subject of the first part of *The Green Shore* appropriately titled *The Rocks,* and focused upon the area of Hodbarrow Point and the old, stone-built lighthouse there.

The old lighthouse still stands, but no evidence remains of any other buildings having existed in its vicinity. However, around fifty years ago, a few cottages really did stand near the lighthouse, one of which probably inspired the fictional Pengwilly cottage. The old lighthouse in reality had originally been built in 1866. In 1905, in connection with the Hodbarrow sea barrier works, it was replaced as a working lighthouse by a steel structure. A ruinous stone-built windmill also still stands nearby as well as an Ordnance Survey triangulation column.

Norman Nicholson

was born in 1914, at Millom, Cumberland, where he still lives. He first became known in 1945, as the editor of the *Penguin Anthology of Modern Religious Verse*. Since then he has published poetry and criticism, and is specially interested in the verse-drama. His play, *The Old Man of the Mountains*, the story of Elijah set in present-day Cumberland, was first produced by Martin Browne at the Mercury Theatre in his series *Plays by Poets*. He has recently published a book about Cumberland and Westmorland, and a study of H. G. Wells. At present he is at work on a book about the Lake District and its literary associations which is to be published by John Lehmann Ltd.

This bookplate was found inside a copy of Nicholson's 1951 biography of William Cowper which clearly had once been part of the library of his friend and mentor, the Rev. Sam Taylor. The other two are images of the young author Nicholson which were featured in some of his earlier published books.

Helen Sutherland's former house at Dockray, above Ullswater, Cockley Moor along with a view of the precipitous road to Martindale Vicarage, at the opposite side of Ullswater, where Kathleen Raine once lived during World War II.

(Pictures by Judith Gale)

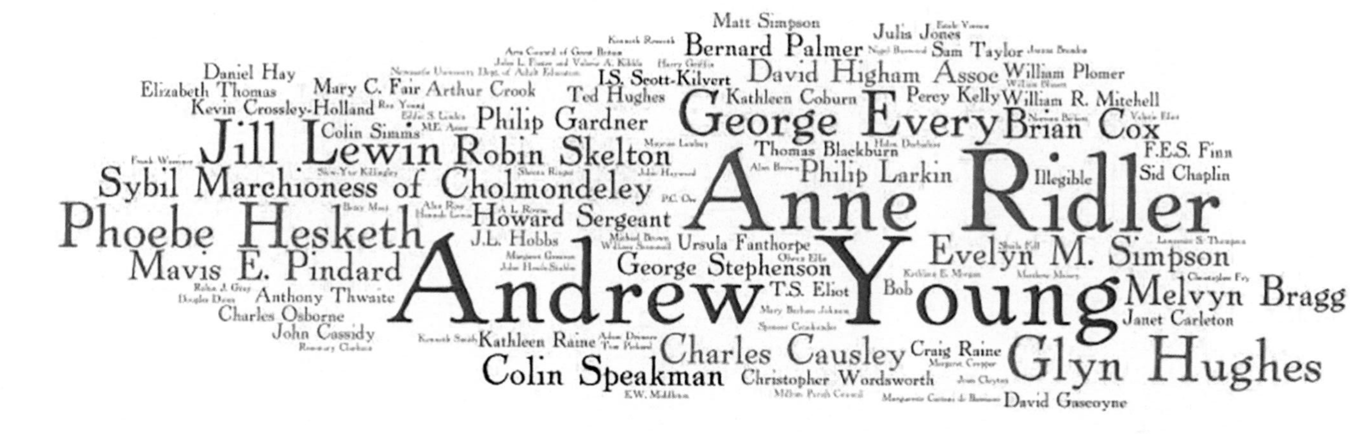

Word Cloud displaying the Names of Nicholson's Correspondents (the 100 most frequent names in his surviving correspondence)

(Reproduced by kind permission of the researchers / compilers, Dr. Christopher Donaldson and Dr. Patricia Murrleta-Flores)

An old snapshot of the young Enrica Garnier, along with a present-day image of Pontesford House in Shropshire, where Enrica was placed in charge of evacuated young Walthamstow Hall School girl pupils.

(Enrica snapshot reproduced with permission; Pontesford House picture by David Boyd)

Headstone of Norman and Yvonne Nicholson's grave in St. George's Churchyard, Millom, aptly overlooking Nicholson's beloved Millom Cricket Field.

(Picture by David Boyd)

Millom Ironworks (painted c. 1960) as it once was, now with only mountains of waste slag left remaining, save poignantly for the solidified and immovable final contents of one of its giant blast furnaces.

(Photos by Judith Gale, Painting by D Tattersall)

Linford Sanatorium, as it was c. 1920, from old postcards.

(Images by kind permission of Mr. Alwyn Ladell)

Nicholson's modest Millom home, 14 St George's Terrace, which he occupied nearly all his life (the memorial plaque now somewhat tarnished).

Pictures by Judith Gale

9

The Plays

Nicholson's first published play was *The Old Man of the Mountains* (Faber and Faber Ltd., 1946). It had originally been commissioned by E. Martin Browne (1900-1980) for his Pilgrim Players towards the end of the War[188]. The play had originally been intended for Pilgrim Players' performances on tour, to be staged within small village and church and community halls. But Browne in 1945 selected Nicholson's play to open a season of 'New Plays by Poets', at the tiny 136-seat Mercury Theatre in London's Notting Hill.

Browne, in his memoirs[189], recounts that his own prior links with George Every had led to Nicholson travelling from Millom to nearby Ulverston to see a wartime performance there of Eliot's play, *Murder in the Cathedral* and that both he and Nicholson '*found ourselves at one in having a special love for the Elijah story*'[190], Nicholson already having the germ of an idea for a verse play about it.

The formal commissioning of that play grew from the seed first planted at the Ulverston meeting. It came into full bloom when Eliot and Nicholson sat together as guests of honour at the play's opening night at the Mercury Theatre, in 1945. In an anecdote that must have come from Nicholson himself, Eliot reportedly sat in impassive silence throughout the performance, and maintained the same demeanour when it ended. Nicholson had become increasingly nervous, throughout, probably highly fearful of the eminent man's disapproval. At last, Eliot got up from his seat to depart, and turned to Norman, saying gruffly:

Promising, Nicholson - Promising!

Then, without another word, Eliot departed into the night[191]

Looking back upon his own *oeuvre,* when interviewed many years later, for local radio[192], Nicholson spoke with evident pride about the success of his very first play, though he did comment that, in hindsight, it had been rather too overtly religious in theme, certainly for modern times and tastes.

But, Nicholson's first play had been very much a product of its own time; part of that wartime and post-war resurgence of medieval forms of didactic religious drama, aimed at ordinary people, and emulating T.S. Eliot's iconic verse play, *Murder in the Cathedral.* In 1929, the Religious Drama Society[193] had been formed by Olive Stevenson, who was the widow of a prominent Congregational churchman. She had persuaded Sir Francis Younghusband, the explorer, to join her. Younghusband had become the Society's first Chairman and Mrs Stevenson the Secretary. The inaugural President was the recently appointed

Bishop of Chichester, George Bell (1883-1958)[194]; Sybil Thorndike was the Vice-President.

Martin Browne, having been appointed in 1930 Diocesan Director of Religious Drama by Bishop Bell, had first collaborated with Eliot regarding the choruses to link the various scenes of *The Rock* , a (1934) pageant, held in Canterbury Cathedral, for the purpose of raising funds for building new Anglican churches to minister to the inhabitants of London's expanding suburbs. The following year was earmarked for the Canterbury Festival, and Bell invited Eliot to write a verse play to be presented there, under the direction of Martin Browne. This play subsequently was given the title *Murder in the Cathedral*. It starred Robert Speaight as Becket, and, following its performance at the Festival, in Canterbury Cathedral's Chapter House, it moved to London, where it ran remarkably successfully for nearly a year; later in 1938 the play transferred to New York.

In 1939, Browne directed Eliot's second play, *The Family Reunion*. In the same year he established, with the aid of an Arts Council[195] grant, a touring company of actors which he named the Pilgrim Players. Following VE Day, in 1945 the Mercury Theatre became the home base and headquarters of the Pilgrim Players, and thus the venue for Nicholson's London stage debut as a verse dramatist.

The theme of *The Old Man of the Mountains* is the Old Testament story of Elijah, transposed from Biblical times in Palestine to the recent past and into the landscape of Nicholson's own familiar and beloved Cumberland.

This kind of approach mirrors some of Nicholson's early poems from *Five Rivers*, especially *The Bow in the Cloud* which, via a similar transposition, recounts the Biblical Noah's Ark story[196]. A few years later, in a (1951) BBC Third Programme broadcast and subsequent article in *The Listener,* entitled *Millom Delivered*, Nicholson explained his transmutation of his home locality into the setting of the Holy Land:

> *....The more I thought of it, the closer the parallel seemed. There were the two hills, of height unlike, the church on one, the devil's boulder on the other; there, behind, were the uplands and the hillside woods; there, to the east, the Duddon, for the Jordan, and to the west, the Irish Sea for the Mediterranean – the Midland Sea, as Fairfax calls it. Above all, there was the desert – the dry, sandy, barren desert of the old mines, out of which the town and the furnaces blossomed like the rose, even though it was an iron rose...*

Grafted onto the Biblical story of Elijah were Nicholson's own, non-Biblical, contemporary, socio-political and ecological concerns, both associated with the (evil, capitalist, environmentally-irresponsible) prominent local landowner, Ahab, and his false God, Baal. In relation to the present-day fears about Man gravely upsetting the balance of Nature this aspect of the Play was remarkably far ahead of its time: the voice of the Raven which was played by Browne himself spoke up with violent and vivid imagery:

...You tear the crops like hair from the living skin;
You drive the earth like a slave; you wring
The last drop of blood from the land till the soil is dried into dust.
The hills which were your altars have become your middens;
The becks[197] *which were your temples have become your sewers...*

The role of the Raven, too, departs from the Biblical story: the bird makes Elijah recognise the value of everyday life or work as valid praise of God as opposed to the emptiness of mere celebratory or ceremonial praise which Elijah had hitherto thought the only possible way to worship. This comparison of the 'contemplative' and the 'active' life is not particularly any component of the Biblical Elijah stories, but it does chime very loudly with further content of Nicholson's *'Millom Delivered' Listener* article, which incorporated Charles Williams' similar theological views.

The Play was generally well received by the critics and was almost universally praised for the overall freshness and effectiveness of its diction. However, a significant flaw in the dramatic structure revealed itself almost from the outset[198], once stage performances began. As the *Times Literary Supplement's* reviewer put it:

... (it) slips in the third act into disastrous anti-climax[199].

Or, as Martin Browne in far more measured tone expressed it:

> *'… (the) play had a structural problem which it took this production to solve…On stage, at this point*[200]*, the play ceased to be convincing.*

The essence of the problem lay in setting and then effectively staging a credible yet climactic ending to the drama, in the form of its Third Act, which originally was set upon the summit of 'Carmel Fell' and involved a somewhat bizarre form of altar-to-altar confrontation between the Baal-worshippers and Elijah's faction, culminating in God miraculously sending rain to end the severe drought previously visited by God upon the heathen Baal-worshippers of the Dale.

Nicholson quickly returned to Millom in order to work upon a complete rewrite of Act Three, which was incorporated into future productions[201] and by Faber and Faber into a revised (1950) Third Impression of the published play. Before that, the play had toured to at least six locations, during 1946 and 1947. Many provincial amateur theatre groups also staged the play, including a run by Workington's (amateur) Playgoers, at the town's Theatre Royal in December, 1946, directed by Workington Grammar School's senior English Teacher and pioneer Lakeland rock climber, Bert Beck or 'Sammy Beck', as was his School nickname.

Workington Playgoers Club had been founded by

prominent local solicitor, Euan Banner Mendus, who was also one of the avant garde Lake District rock climbers and a driving force behind the sailing club at Bassenthwaite Lake. Nicholson was to be guest of honour at one of the performances and stayed the night with the recently married Banner-Mendus couple in order to allow him adequate respite from the rigours of the journey from Millom. The former Mrs Banner-Mendus recalls facing the culinary challenge of providing Nicholson with a palatable light meal before the performance; she had decided upon a fish dish, which Nicholson praised for '*its very jolly little sauce*'.[202]

Workington's amateur actors are unlikely to have found any difficulty convincingly enunciating the distinctive, Norse-derived, dialect of Cumberland, unlike the play's cast of actors at the Mercury Theatre production. Martin Browne, in his autobiography, recalls that they were so unaccustomed and uncomfortable with the dialect that he had to enlist the help of his friend, Miss Margaret Cropper (1886-1980), as their dialect coach. Browne had once staged some of Margaret Cropper's religious plays during the early 1930s; she was a prolific poet, hymn writer and a truly formidable local community figure. Margaret was one of the Cropper papermaking dynasty, from Burneside, near Kendal, in Westmorland.[203]

Nicholson, thirty-five years later, in an affectionate obituary to Margaret Cropper[204] mentioned her exceptional ability to capture in verse both the tone and the idiom of Westmorland dialect speech without resorting to dropped letters and phonetic spellings - a skill which Nicholson observed had eluded Wordsworth, who had made even his most bucolic Westmorland characters speak unconvincingly in standard King's English.

Margaret Cropper, remarkably, published her last book of poetry (in fact, jointly with some of Nicholson's)[205] at the age of ninety-two. Nicholson recalled in his obituary a poetry reading at Brewery Arts in Kendal when she, a very old lady by then, was persuaded to read aloud to the audience one of her own poems. This the ninety-three-year-old lady did, and impeccably too: it was an extremely moving moment, he recalled.

Another attempt to improve the realism of the Play's dialect probably led to the decision to cast a Millom amateur actor as Ahab: on August 25, 1945, the local newspaper the *West Cumberland News* reported:

MILLOM PLAY and MILLOM ACTOR

The cast of Mr Norman Nicholson's play "The Old Man of the Mountains" which is to be produced in London on September 13 is to include Mr Richmond B Ward, the well-known and talented Millom amateur actor.

Mr Ward is to play opposite Robert Speaight as Ahab to his Elijah; in this case the Biblical characters being portrayed as a rather rascally Cumberland squire and a small fell farmer. Mr Ward has already gone to London to take part in rehearsals.

Another reason behind this casting decision may have been that Browne's Pilgrim Players had a tradition of using amateur actors, as part of their need to operate upon shoestring budgets.

Henry Reed reviewed the Mercury's first run of the play enthusiastically for *The Listener*[206], making no mention of anything being wrong with the Third Act, and finding it an 'infinitely more attractive' play than Robert Duncan's *This Way to the Tomb*.

Reed's review concluded glowingly:

> *The play is apparently a first effort in drama; but it is an enormously promising one, and it is to be hoped that Mr Nicholson will soon attempt a play with a plot of his own invention.*

The Old Man of the Mountains continued subsequently to be regularly performed both throughout the U.K. and beyond, including once being staged within the ruins of the bomb-destroyed Coventry Cathedral. Other performances took place in Denmark, New York, U.S.A., and in Christchurch, in New Zealand.[207] In 1955, too, this Play (presumably by then translated into Welsh) won First Prize at the Pwllheli National Eisteddfod of Wales in 1955.

Nicholson's second play, *Prophesy to the Wind*, was also a commission, this time in 1947, by the Little Theatre Guild of Great Britain, a Federation of small, amateur theatres and acting companies which had been formally constituted in 1946. The Guild had in fact stipulated to Nicholson that the play should be set in a post-atomic age[208], doubtless having been deeply influenced by the cataclysmic unleashing of nuclear bombs upon Hiroshima and Nagasaki. The play was first performed at the Newcastle People's Theatre in January, 1949, and was first published by Faber and Faber in 1950.

The play was decidedly on a theme of Nicholson's own invention, as opposed to the retelling of a Biblical story. However, Nicholson still chose to set the play within his native Cumberland, and chose the principal characters to match. The play was about the aftermath of a nuclear war when the survivors from it had reverted to the bygone social and economic structures of their ancient, Viking ancestors. One principal character was given the name Hallbjorn, whence Nicholson presumably speculated that the place name for old Millom - Holborn Hill - had originally derived. Similarly, the name of the play's brother of Hallbjorn, Ulf clearly links with Cumbrian place names such as Ullswater and Ulpha. The play's actual location setting is called *'Hallbjorn Hill*[209]*, on the north-west coast of England'*, and the time is set *'in the future.'*

The title of the Play retained some distinct Biblical affiliations, from the wording of Ezekiel 37:9:

> *Then said he unto me, Prophesy unto the wind, prophesy, son of man, and say to the wind, Thus saith the Lord God; Come from the four winds, O breath, and breathe upon these slain, that they may live.*

The wider Biblical story appropriately sets Ezekiel in a valley awash with the dry bones of long-dead multitudes, which God demonstrates that He can readily equip once more with flesh and blood and miraculously bring back to life. It echoes, too, perhaps, some of T.S. Eliot's arid and despairing imagery from *The Waste Land*._

During the 1950s, Nicholson became well acquainted with Carlisle's amateur theatre company, known as The Green Room Club. In January 1956, the Club (who themselves joined the Little Theatre Guild in 1985) staged *Prophesy to the Wind* at their relatively new West Walls Theatre for which Gardner, in his thesis, indicates that Nicholson himself contributed the Programme Notes, and quotes from these at fair length. Unfortunately, though, the original notes do not seem to have survived.

Nicholson's notes outlined his theory that isolated, remote areas of Europe, such as Iceland or the Faroes or Scandinavia might possibly escape being wholly wiped out by any worldwide nuclear war and might following such an event spread out to rebuild a form of civilisation in some of the devastated regions. He imagines his native southwest Cumberland as having been re-colonised by surviving Danes, the descendants of Viking settlers, having reverted to their ancestral simple subsistence farming in harsh environments.

In summary, the play's plot involves an old man, Hallbjorn; Ulf, his swaggering brother, a shepherd and Vikar, their kinsman; Freya. Hallbjorn's daughter, Freya provides the love-interest; others in the cast are Freya's maid, Bessie; Dick, a charcoal-burner whilst the dramatic contrast to all of this group is John, an engineer who has time-travelled from the pre-war, industrialised era.

The play opens with a Prologue which outlines this post-war scenario to the audience. Prior to John's unexpected appearance on the scene, Vikar had been all set to marry Freya; Hallbjorn generally welcomes this plan, but Freya and John subsequently meet and, of course, the two fall deeply in love, to Vikar's violent resentment.

Four Scenes follow, which lead to the off-stage slaying of John by Vikar, and a largely unhappy ending to the drama, which therefore might loosely, overall, be classified as falling within the *genre* of Tragedy.

This, Nicholson's first attempt at modern, secular, futuristic, even 'science fiction' drama was not too successful, although *The Listener*, reviewing it alongside contemporaneous new plays by Robert Duncan and Christopher Fry, considered his efforts to be 'both sounder than Mr Duncan and more serious than Mr Fry'[210].

There is even some indication that TS Eliot himself considered the play to be 'a real technical advance'[211] (although the correspondence containing the primary evidence for this was destroyed, Gardner's thesis cites Eliot's favourable opinions as having been set out in a particular letter from Nicholson to George Every, written c. April, 1949).

Nonetheless, *Prophesy to the Wind* has not escaped almost total obscurity as one of the most forgotten of all of Nicholson's plays. But all Nicholson's plays reflect his poetry, and *vice versa.* For example, Nicholson's whimsical yet fine and deadly serious poem *Gathering Sticks on Sunday* from his 1954 Collection *The Pot Geranium* imagines the 'Man in the Moon' looking skywards at the beautiful shape of Earth, (with prophetic foresight of the exploration of space and such as the 1969 American lunar landing) and being startled to see big changes to its surface - giant pockmarks of vast (nuclear bomb) craters where green and verdant land and abundant life had formerly been apparent:

> *...He'll know that soon*
> *The living world of men*
> *Will take a lunar look, as dead as slag,*
> *And moon and earth will stare at one another*
> *Like the cold, yellow skulls of child and mother.*

'*As dead as slag'* in particular is an oft-used and symbolic Nicholson image: it recurs word for word in Hallbjorn's haunting description in *Prophesy to the Wind* of the lifeless and lethal aridity of all the land nearer the sites of the nuclear explosions:

> *...you come across a country where the land / is dead as slag or cinders / Not even a rat /lives there: a worm, a snake; not even a bird flies over...*[212]

The dichotomy between the rock of Nicholson's God-made Earth and the dead man-made industrial waste that formed the slagheap which encroached almost up to many Millom residents' home doorsteps is both vivid and enduring, as well as being pervasive throughout Nicholson's works.

Sexual content creeps into Nicholson's later plays, starting with *Prophesy to the Wind*, in which Freya and John fall deeply in love. Later in the play it is revealed by a distraught Freya to her father and to John's murderer, Vikar, that she is in fact carrying John's baby, which adds further tragic poignancy to the drama.

Nicholson's next play reverted to a Biblical setting, but retained a measure of love interest and sexual content, being the story of Hosea and his wife, a temple prostitute, and it was published as *A Match for the Devil* in 1955.[213]

According to Gardner's thesis, as early as 1951, Nicholson had been reading the Old Testament Book of Hosea, and finding it 'a valuable new experience'[214] Possible parallels between Nicholson's personal life and his literary works and their themes have already been speculatively discussed in the context of his novels[215] Exactly how Nicholson found the theme 'valuable' to him of course remains unexplained but, evidently, in some way he very much did.

There are further obvious connections made in Nicholson's article for *The Listener*, titled *The Comic Prophet*[216], which itself supplements his *Millom Delivered* talk and *The Listener* transcript of a year earlier[217]. In particular, Nicholson returns to his imaginary transposition of Millom and its locality (and the wider England) into Biblical Palestine.

Another article which Nicholson wrote in 1952 for the periodical *Time and Tide,* about Man's need for ritual through all the ages and in all societies stated that:

> *...Gradually, the more primitive processes were abandoned. The great religions emerged, the cult of temple prostitution was transformed in the shining eyes of Hosea into the Sacred Marriage ofYaweh and His people...*[218].

This perhaps summarises Nicholson's overall view of the theme of his forthcoming play, *A Match for the Devil*: that the Hosea bible story was symbolic of God's infinite and compassionate love for His people.

Nicholson was to pay a high price for offending entrenched contemporary codes of conventional morality by writing a religious drama within a context of prostitution and adultery, and all in a rather comic manner. This play had originally been commissioned by the Religious Drama Society, specifically for staging in its north of England region by their newly appointed regional co-ordinator, Pamela Keily, in collaboration with E. Martin Browne.

Gardner, in his thesis, relates that Browne had passed on to Nicholson the commission for a play for a new company of (Northern England) touring professionals, to perform. The target audiences would be (typically) industrial-town 'Church' audiences - not necessarily all of them being devout Church activists, but generally more diverse audiences than had been intended for *The Old Man of the Mountains.*

E. Martin Browne rather imprudently but of course not at the time blessed with the benefit of hindsight had cut corners somewhat, and mistakenly had assumed the Religious Drama Society would inevitably fully approve the play. Gardner explains that Browne, in order to save a lot of wasted time, had by-passed the Religious Drama Society's Head Office approval process by directly passing Nicholson's part-completed play to Pamela Keily and her company of Northern Players (who had immediately started rehearsals of the available content) and only retrospectively submitting it to the Religious Drama Society Executive Committee for formal approval.

However, when the suitability of the play was called into question, Browne, as Chairman of the Society, and of the Executive Committee had taken the most unusual step of asking that a verbatim report of that Special Executive Committee Meeting be taken: fortunately, this report remains available in the Society's archives, enabling the detailed facts at last to emerge.[219]

That Special Meeting took place at S.P.C.K. House in London on 11 February, 1953. In addition to Martin Browne and his wife Henzie, five Committee members were present, including the Cambridge academic and religious playwright, Mrs K.M. Baxter. Six Committee members submitted their Apologies; the record indicates that copies of Nicholson's programme note for the play had been circulated beforehand. The Chairman opened the Meeting, authoritatively, thus:

This is a special meeting, which has been called at the request of a number of members to discuss A MATCH FOR THE DEVIL. It would save time to recall the circumstances of the origin of the play. When we formed the New Pilgrims, the great problem was to find enough suitable plays to start them on their way - HOLY FAMILY was the only play that we already had laid on. We set about trying to commission plays, Mrs Baxter wrote T'OTHER SHIFT, which is very successful for the particular purpose for which it was meant. We also agreed that we should invite the Pilgrim Players Ltd. to commission a full-length play from Norman Nicholson, and A MATCH FOR THE DEVIL is the result. The play has been written against time, and we have had to deal with it in pieces, as we have received it, and the Executive, has only now had a chance to read it. Although the New Pilgrims are already advanced in preparation of the play, it would not be right for them to present it if the Executive feels it is wrong to do so. This must be decided at this meeting,

I think the best thing to do will be to go round the room, asking people to put their views for or against. Let us try not to duplicate what we say. I have asked for a verbatim report of this meeting to be taken…

We learn that pressure from 'a number of Society members' had led to the Meeting being convened.

Henzie Browne opened the Committee members' comments by praising the play, in itself, but nonetheless asserting that there was a *'major uncertainty'* in her mind as to her support for it, because the presentation of the Temple as a place of ritual prostitution whilst at the same time a centre for sincere religious worship would be likely to be *'bewildering'* to audiences.

Mrs Baxter thought the Play nothing at all like religious drama, but '*quite an amusing salacious comedy with some very funny lines*', and she said that audiences would misunderstand '*the Church as being the Temple, and Gomer as a modern, 'common' prostitute rather than as a ritual, religious one from a bygone era.'*

The clergymen present at the meeting unanimously echoed their total opposition to the play's religious prostitution theme, in spite of the fact that it was in the distant past and the whole purpose was didactic as opposed to mere entertainment, adding their personal feelings of outrage at Nicholson's departures from the actual Old Testament content and storyline.

Pamela Keily read to the Meeting extracts from a letter she had received from Nicholson about the play. Nicholson must have been immensely hurt and affronted by all this officious and censorious treatment, but his response given the circumstances remained remarkably polite and measured. He painstakingly explained his didactic intent, which he said was *'to catch audiences off their guard, that is, as it were, wearing their week-day consciences.'* At first, the audience is encouraged by Nicholson to sympathise with Hosea and his difficulties with Gomer; then to join in sympathy with the shallow, conventional, judgemental characters who make fun of and deride Hosea, the cuckold. But then, the audience is led to readjust their sympathies to see things through the eyes of the newly-enlightened Hosea and fully to realise just how totally inadequate had been their original 'kneejerk' responses based on of their ingrained, conventional, unquestioned attitudes.

Interestingly, Nicholson compared this technique with that ofT.S. Eliot, in *The Cocktail Party.* Nicholson seems to have adopted here a very typical Eliotic dialectical theme – involving arriving back at where one started, but, as a consequence of the journey, knowing the starting place for the first time.

Pamela Keily herself much later recalled these events[220]:

On our move to Leeds it seemed wise to have morning rehearsals and the governing body had commissioned Norman to write for us. He too had come to visit me in Sheffield before the company had assembled and was in the throes of writing a play about Hosea and Amos, with the requisite number of characters for the New Pilgrims. Unfortunately, bad health meant delay over the arrival of the script.

Two acts had been written by the time we went into rehearsal in Leeds. The company were enchanted by this new play with its sensitive and charming verse. We started without having the complete script. Suddenly, with the eventual completion of act three, there came a summons to London for the director.

We were all of us thrilled by the rehearsals of this wholly new creation but it seemed to strike the governing body as something that would hurt and shock the audience by its interpretation of the scriptures. Only Martin Browne gave it support when I went to that meeting in London. I was told not to go ahead, and I still remember the incredible sense of Martin's sympathy as he saw me off at Kings Cross[221].

I had to break the news to the company and knew the disappointment could well lead to a breakup of the group…

…The hurt in the author on having his play turned down was acute. As a Christian poet of distinction he felt as if he was being treated as though he wrote for the sea-side pier. I hope we redeemed the situation when he was commissioned years later by the Northern Provincial Committee for Religious Drama to write Birth by Drowning.

The front page of *The Church Times* of Friday 10 April 1953 made public these stark facts:

RELIGIOUS PLAY WITHDRAWN

The Religious Drama Society of Great Britain withdrew a specially written play which was to have been performed at Sheffield YWCA recently. The performance was withdrawn on the grounds that the Biblical subject was

> *not portrayed with true theological values. The production was called A Match for the Devil. The author is Mr Norman Nicholson. The players performed instead, Henri Gheon's Way of the Cross, at St. Paul's, Arbour-thorne.*

Pamela Keily's recollections of the force and intensity of E. Martin Browne's objections do not seem fully to reflect the recorded facts of the matter. Browne's wife, Henzie, for example, shared the same strong reservations as all the other members of the whole chorus of objectors. Browne himself does not come across in the verbatim record of the committee meeting as a very vociferous or robust opponent of the objections, but seems to have been choosing his mildly-contradictory words very carefully. For example, he commented:

> *'To me, what he (Nicholson) says in the programme note makes it quite clear that he is trying to put over something that we really want to have said.'*

With little or no further serious opposition on his part, Browne as Chairman urged the meeting to select a 'safe' alternative play from elsewhere, and, exercising his Chairmanly impartiality without further ado, Browne allowed the meeting 'unanimously' to vote for the withdrawal of R.D.S. sponsorship from the play.

Following this unexpected, rebuff from the play's sponsors, Gardner recounts, in his thesis, that Nicholson and his associates strenuously tried to rescue the work from total extinction. Ultimately, it was chosen for staging at the Edinburgh Festival (St Mary's Hall) by the London Club Theatre Group, where its first performance took place on 28 August, 1953[222] *The Sunday Times* reported that *'the Play has been well received here'*[223], although their reviewer admitted to have been personally unimpressed, in particular by its diction. Muriel Spark happened that year to be reporting on the Festival for the *Church of England Newspaper (CEN).* Her review of *Match for the Devil* appeared in *CEN* of 4 September, 1953, where she describes the cast as performing 'with due vigour', and observed that:

The play deals with the matrimonial career of the prophet Hosea, who the author claims in a foreword on the programme 'was one of the first of the prophets to see the relation between God and Man as one of love rather than law[224], in terms indeed, of a divine marriage between God and His people, at the centre of which lay 'forgiveness'.

Muriel Spark opined that Nicholson's notes failed to be reflected in the actual play, which she said was the fault of the notes rather than any fault of the play. The play, however, she thought too forcefully didactic to be successful, lacking in the art of suggestion.

Significantly, none of these critics' reviews raised even the tiniest reservations about any moral or theological impropriety about the play.

Amongst the audience at that Edinburgh production had been a group of Overseas Theatre Group students from Denison University, Granville, Ohio, USA who wrote to their academic tutor in high praise of this new play. The result was that this Nicholson play was given its first American performance at the Denison University Theatre, later in 1953.[225]

The play went on to a performance in Manchester by The Unnamed Society, in June, 1954. *The Manchester Guardian* reviewer awarded it a small measure of praise, but criticised it for 'a yawning lack of action'[226]. Faber ultimately published the play in 1955, and in that format it was fairly well-received by *The Times Literary Supplement's* reviewer, as:

> *...with all its faults...lively reading and well worth the attention of repertory companies.*[227]

However, there is no record of any further productions having been staged beyond 1954, with the notable exception of a performance in Wakefield some twenty or more years later, which Pamela Keily recalled 'received the encouraging reactions of light-hearted enjoyment from the audience, as the author originally intended.'[228] Nicholson's play originally perhaps had been too far ahead of its time. Indeed, one of the reasons for this was penetratingly remarked upon by Pamela Keily:

> *The Christian poet and the theologically minded priest speak two different languages, and one of the numerous headaches in 'religious drama' is trying to please both.*[229]

The very first UK amateur dramatic production of the still-unpublished *A Match for the Devil* was in October, 1954 by the same Green Room Club of Carlisle, which, subsequently, two years later, performed *Prophesy to the Wind*[230]. Nicholson travelled from Millom to Carlisle to be guest of honour at the first night of the former, and he addressed the audience at the end of the performance, in particular praising the way the producer had interpreted his play.[231]

Comedy - sometimes sheer slapstick - was a feature of *A Match for the Devil*, as well as graphic and sometimes overtly suggestive language. But, in a further, significant, way, when viewed in a context somewhat wider than that of 'safe', conventional, somewhat sanctimonious post-war religious drama, this play can be seen as having been extremely 'modern' and progressive for its day. In particular, Nicholson's own, non-Biblical, portrayal of Hosea and his spirited wife, Gomer's relationship, and of their eventual reconciliation as a couple, was daringly innovative, both in its affirmative tone and its support of the notion that women and wives deserved very much more autonomy and equality and respect from a male-dominated Society. On its own, the Old Testament story, in line with ancient traditions of female subjugation, virtually ignores Gomer as a person in her own right, focusing exclusively upon the man / her husband, Hosea.

Nicholson, from early on in the play's gestation[232], recognised acutely that the Biblical story itself contained no credible dramatic reason why Gomer should decide to return to her husband, so he endowed her with the attitude of a modern, liberated, woman, who was indignant and angry at Hosea's patronising offer to 'forgive' her, on the basis that, from her side of it, there was nothing to forgive, and she therefore refuses to be treated like:

> *...a dirty cup to be rinsed out and set on the shelf again.*

Gomer refuses to return on Hosea's original terms of one-sided and selfish assurances of his own forgiveness of her and of his love for her: she realises that it is she who matters too. It dawns on Gomer that the whole arrangement ought to be a reciprocal one, and that the purest and most genuine manifestations of human love can sometimes be a joyous, even comic, glimpse of God's own, infinite love.[233], '

In 1957, Pamela Keily, on behalf of the Committee for Religious Drama in the Northern Province[234] commissioned a new play by Nicholson, which he accepted, in spite of his humiliating treatment a few years previously by Pamela Keily's paymasters. The play was to be performed in the open air, by a large cast of theology student amateur actors, and to form part of the 1959 commemoration festivities of the Community for the Resurrection at Mirfield in Yorkshire, to be staged in a vast outdoor arena - a former quarry, and in front of an audience of about four thousand people.

The Community's Quarry Theatre is now disused, and the tradition of the annual play was abandoned in 1972,[235] but there are presently (as at Summer, 2013) plans going forward to restore it, with the collaboration of Opera North and Huddersfield Choral Society and to reopen with a first performance in Summer 2014.[236]

The commission may have been by way of making some belated amends for Nicholson's earlier treatment by the Religious Drama Society, but the times were changing in any event: shortly after the first performance of *Birth by Drowning*, in July, 1959, the *Lady Chatterley's Lover* trial at the Old Bailey was to transform traditional UK Establishment attitudes towards public morality and censorship.

The Mirfield performance of *Birth by Drowning* was thus an integral part of a far wider religious spectacle and spiritual festival and celebration: it was not by any means a mere theatrical event, staged under the roof of a mere theatre. *The Church Times* [237] reported that buses filled with people from just about every parish in the north of England had been arriving from early morning at this small southwest Yorkshire town.[238] They had packed into the Anglican Monastery's large church for a service of High Mass, then spread themselves all over the grounds and the lawns to eat their picnic lunches, until around 5pm the throng drifted towards that Quarry Theatre, which *The Church Times* correspondent deftly and vividly described as:

> *...a natural hollow of considerable magnitude, like a great Roman theatre, admirably sheltered from the Yorkshire*

> *winds and subjected to no disturbances other than the rustling of foliage and the distant tooting of trains...*

The Church Times correspondent had clearly enjoyed every aspect of the play - especially Nicholson's three talking-mountains:

> *The three mountains, to whom was owed so much both of humour and grandeur, were symbolized by John Cant, David Warner and John Blackburn. These mountains skipped like rams. When they had caustic and confidential things to say to each other they got down from their eminences and came closer, though carefully keeping the right proportion of distance between themselves. Each had its own character, as mountains do. All were quite vocally gifted...*

Birth by Drowning was to be the last of Nicholson's published plays, and it is generally the least esteemed, critically. On the surface, at least, it represents a revamp of *The Old Man of the Mountains.* The Holy Land is transposed to Cumberland; the central character is both from the Old Testament, and indeed is Elijah's successor, Elisha.

But, underneath this surface veneer, this play differed greatly from its predecessors. It was a play written to meet special, if not unique, demands and constraints, the commissioning brief from Pamela Keily being for:

> *...a play which (could) be enjoyed by some three to four thousand folk of 'bank holiday' texture.* [239]

A religious play for the entertainment of '*not-over-sophisticated*' audiences [240] was required, and, therefore, it is unrealistic to expect the result to be anything other than intellectually rather lightweight and largely devoid of any profundity.

Faber published the play in 1960, and it was reviewed with some apparent distaste by the poet Patric Dickinson (1914-1994) in *The Times Literary Supplement.*[241] Nicholson's unconventional and innovative adoption of three Cumbrian mountain peaks as the Chorus (so loved by *The Church Times* reviewer) was considered to be '*ludicrous*' by Dickinson and the Cumberland setting '*not very satisfactory*' and the re-telling of the Biblical Elisha story '*taking liberties of an un-aesthetic nature.*'

Pamela Keily herself makes no comment either way about the play in her memoirs, although she does mention therein that her own Sheffield cast of players did, post-Mirfield, perform it elsewhere in that area[242] and she refers to an (undated) favourable local newspaper's review of a 1960 performance of the play in Carver Street Methodist Hall.[243] The endorsement of the play by the Bishop of Wakefield, is reported by Nicholson[244] himself, the Bishop is said to have commented that the commissioning of the play had been vindicated - and '*magnificently*'. On this occasion at least, even the least progressive of the religious drama world seemed well pleased with the outcome of their latest Nicholson commission.

But there were to be no further Nicholson plays following *Birth by Drowning*, and, as plays, they remain, like his novels, seldom visited almost completely neglected backwaters of his mainstream literary work. Gardner, in his 1969/1970 thesis discussed at some length both the novels and the plays, but chose to ignore Nicholson's considerable journalistic output and topographical prose. David Cooper's 2007 thesis on Nicholson and Place and Space has already been mentioned in the context of Nicholson's plays; he observes thus:[245]:

> *Gardner...places considerable emphasis on Nicholson's achievement as a dramatist, dedicating a chapter to the examination of the four Christian verse plays: works whose imaginative limitations upon the page have been reflected in their negligible performance histories. He also consciously marginalizes Nicholson's topographical writing, dismissing the regional prose books as 'peripheral' and 'discursive and descriptive rather than creative'. My thesis reverses Gardner's critical position: in the following chapters, the four verse plays are pushed to one side and, instead, greater attention is awarded to Nicholson's topographical prose books and his other works of non-fiction dedicated to the exploration of landscape and environment.*

Whilst *Prophesy to the Wind* might not be too appropriately described as 'Christian', it is nonetheless plain that the themes of Nicholson's plays were generally and predominantly exactly that. They were products of their particular period and age, and perhaps inevitably seem outmoded and simplistically didactic to present day tastes.

Nonetheless, it remains absolute that Nicholson was a poet first and a verse dramatist second. His interest in verse drama can be seen not only as treading in the footsteps of Eliot but also as a means of promulgating his poetry in particular, and in promoting his art and indeed his Christian faith in general, to an audience far wider and more inclusive of all classes of Society than conventional poetry collections in printed books could ever reach.

Nicholson wrote at some length about this particular notion as early as in a literary magazine article of 1948[246]. With a typically magnificent concluding flourish, he ended his piece thus:

> *...I cannot speak for London, for I know little of the London theatre, but I have sat with many Northern audiences, and I feel that these people will not be afraid of poetry nor embarrassed by it if the poet will speak in a language which they can understand and which belongs to the life they know.*

This entire article, although dated, provides deep insight into Nicholson's lifelong mission to perform his poetry to audiences who normally would never come into contact with 'modern' poetry. And even if they did encounter poetry whilst casually browsing books and magazines, their understanding of it would be very seriously constrained by modern reading habits:

> *...On paper the reader can study the shape and substance of the verse, but it does not become a poem till it is alive at his lips or, at least, at his ears. But the poet today writes for a people most of whom have never learned to read. Instead of reading they glance over, and they have developed a sort of visual Braille, by which they recognise the shapes of letters and groups of letters and even of whole phrases and blocks of type without really translating them into words at all. Now this method, which is admirable for the quick gathering of information, is quite useless for reading poetry, yet for the majority, it is the only method they know. They skim through a poem as if they were searching for a name in a telephone directory, and then wonder why they have not understood...*

Sixty-five years have passed since Nicholson first wrote (in current parlance) this 'blog'. Today, the Internet and the media inundate all of us with torrents of words by the million or even billion and Nicholson's distinction between uncomprehending, impressionistic, speed-reading or skimming and 'closer', fuller reading is even more salient in 2014 which may help towards understanding why verse drama has in present times declined almost to the point of extinction.

Nicholson devoted nearly the whole of his adult life to the role of peripatetic reciter of his own verse, in return for which he received little financial reward, often just fairly meagre reimbursement of his actual expenses. It was a role into which he had been born, virtually;

it stretched back to his childhood as the champion boy reciter of the Millom festivals. In spite of his physical frailty and the death of his wife and his own advancing old age, it is hugely notable and worth repeating that Nicholson never gave up his heartfelt and driving mission of striving to bring his poetry to full life in front of audiences of ordinary people, usually in little village halls, church rooms and the like.

The extract below, from an old magazine article further illustrates Nicholson's lifelong, basic literary *credo*, and provides considerable explanation for the way he lived his literary life. His outlook was in essence very much provincial as opposed to cosmopolitan; it was essentially egalitarian and pragmatically didactic: not in any way elitist or obscurely intellectual.

Nicholson took pains to deploy, in his verse drama and in his own recitals and radio broadcasts, methods of bringing poetry to the attention of people who would not ordinarily either read it, or even would not be likely fully to understand it, if they happened to read it in conventional, published-book, form. And, equally if not even more illuminating, are Nicholson's justifications for adopting what was to become his hallmark: colloquial and clear and intelligible poetic style and diction:

> *...if the modern poetic drama addresses itself solely to that public which reads poetry, then it will become weak and etiolated and will never develop into the drama which the theatre so badly needs. This does not mean that*

> *the poet must write down to his audience, but he must be prepared, obviously, to make his words intelligible at the speed at which the listener receives them, and he must provide enough of action, plot and character to keep the whole of the audience entertained and interested even if the deeper significance of his symbolism is missed by some of them, even, perhaps, by most. He is not obliged to write for nitwits, but he should have a reasonable respect for the man who, without special knowledge of modern poetry, is ready to pay his half-crown and listen honestly and attentively. That man is an essential part of any normal audience...*[247]

But Nicholson was also at pains to emphasise that the poet ought not merely to adapt self to the audience but must self-create an audience's potential engagement to which the poet must adapt: the poet should be aware that most audiences are made up of people not necessarily straining at the leash to hear every syllable of the poet's fine words.

Other parts of this article relate to poetic and dramatic diction; Nicholson ascribes to Wordsworth the revolutionary alignment once more of poetry and drama with common speech, as had been the case in Elizabethan times. In modern times, though, contemporary speech and poetic diction had become misaligned to the point of dislocation. Nicholson's prose here typically sparkles with hidden poetic gems of his own, such as this one:

> ***...And Ford [248] could take simple words and lay them side by side like pieces of coloured glass for the light to shine through them:***
>
> *Fernando, in short words, howe'er my tongue*
> *Did often chide thy love, each word thou spak'st*
> *Was music to my ear; was never poor,*
> *Poor wretched woman lived that loved like me,*
> *So truly, so unfeignedly.*

Nicholson perhaps sensed, in a way, that contemporary English drama was diverging: one essentially 'naturalistic' divergence leading towards the kitchen sinks and all the crude realism of the era of the angry young men and another one, based, even if increasingly 'modern', upon the traditional stage drama of Shakespeare and even of the earlier English medieval Mystery Plays which effectively engaged, involved (often didactically) and interacted with the audience at several intellectual levels simultaneously.[249]

Thus, Nicholson's own verse plays, as do his novels, provide invaluable and clear insights into Nicholson's other works, however dated, unloved and forgotten they may now have become. They still, if only for this reason, continue handsomely to repay scrutiny.

10

The Journalism and Other Literary Criticism

Introduction

Apart from receiving a steady income from his book royalties, Nicholson supplemented this with his fees as a freelance journalist and broadcaster. His very first published piece was at the age of ten in 1924 when he won a children's essay prize from his local newspaper. His last was sixty-three years later, in 1987, when the London literary magazine *Aquarius* posthumously[250] published a piece he had written for them about the poetry of the 1940s, which had been the subject of a special issue of that magazine.

Nicholson wrote many hundreds of book reviews for the *TLS* between the years of 1948 and 1983, these peaking in number during the 1960s. Traditionally, the identities of *TLS* reviewers were kept completely anonymous, but the *TLS*'s extensive archives have been digitised and e-published in recent years, these citations for the first time revealing the previously withheld names of the reviewers. Nicholson's own name appears frequently amongst them.

Nicholson once commented that:

> *...I did a vast amount of hack work. Living at home, with no great expenses, not having to provide a house, not having a wife, not having children - what I was making at hack work was quite enough to keep me going. I used to review, particularly in the old anonymous days, for the TLS. I must have reviewed hundreds of books a year, great batches of books, five at a time - travel books, autobiographies, biographies, books about the evangelicals, books about missionaries, books (God knows why) about Africa. I became almost an expert on Africa at one time. And books where the literary and religious would come together: that was my particular speciality...*[251]

'Hundreds of books a year' is probably a slight exaggeration on Nicholson's part, but it is clear that book reviewing was an integral component of his freelance journalism and of his income in general.

In 1943, the Student Christian Movement Press published Nicholson's first prose book, *Man and Literature.* This book is the subject of a separate sub-chapter (which follows this one), so in the meantime we return to discussion of Nicholson's 'jobbing journalism'.

Grateful acknowledgement must be made here to the epic bibliography of all Nicholson's work which was completed in 1992 by Andrew F. Wilson and, sadly, never published, although he most helpfully deposited a reference copy with Whitehaven's County Archives Records Office.

Wilson's meticulous records show that Nicholson wrote mainly about either literature or his beloved Cumberland, or sometimes both. He was a regular contributor to *Time and Tide*, *John O'London's Weekly* and to *The Listener*, all now defunct titles; many of his articles in *The Listener* were transcripts or summaries of programmes which Nicholson had previously broadcast on BBC Radio - either on the Home Service or on the more 'highbrow' BBC Third Programme.[252]

It is fascinating to browse Nicholson's manifold and miscellaneous articles in so very many now-ancient periodicals and to experience that unique, lucid and fresh Nicholson style, but there are so very many of them that one has to be selective in singling out those which shed new or clearer light upon the author himself. It soon becomes apparent too, that Nicholson was adept at grabbing and holding the attention of audiences, even readers of his 'popular periodical' articles, in that he flexed and varied greatly his delivered content and style in order to suit his intended audiences or readers. The content of a particular piece of Nicholson journalism thus does not necessarily reflect clearly Nicholson's own personal *credo* about the matter.

Man and Literature

Nicholson's ambitious early book of literary commentary[253] was, as he emphatically stated in his introduction to it, not a survey of modern literature from a Christian perspective. Nor was it, he claimed in the introduction, really literary criticism of any kind, but rather an enquiry into the various assumptions about Man, or Human Nature, or civilised Life on Earth, which he saw as underpinning most contemporary thought and writing. He contrasted this 'modern' era with the pre-Enlightenment era, throughout which most people had shared a common but deep and universal religious faith and had unquestioningly subscribed to ingrained, traditional church dogma about the nature of Man.

Post-Enlightenment doctrines and assumptions about the nature of Man challenged accepted Christian church ones but they diverged, as Nicholson saw it, into distinct groupings, either of a 'Liberal Man' or a 'Natural Man' persuasion, the former typified by the writings of such as H.G. Wells and the latter principally by the work of D.H. Lawrence.

Amongst the authors who had inspired the book, Nicholson in his Introduction cited Eliot's (1933) lectures *After Strange Gods* along with Nicholson's friend George Every's little book entitled *Christian Discrimination*[254] and their mutual friend S.L. Bethell's similar book, *The Literary Outlook*.[255]

With the significant exception of Queenie Leavis,[256] reviewers reacted very positively indeed to the young

Nicholson's book. The cover 'blurb' quoted *The Church Times* review as commenting:

> *So uniformly good from beginning to end that it may well be called brilliant.*

The Times Literary Supplement's review was somewhat less fulsome in its praise,[257] but, in a long and balanced analysis, their reviewer treated Nicholson's book sympathetically and in some detail, for the most part praising Nicholson's engaging, colloquial style and avoidance of prim solemnity.

Sales of the book must have been correspondingly brisk, for even in the midst of the Second World War[258] a Second Edition was needed after only three months, this Second Edition being published in the January of 1944. However, the initial success of the book was not sustained: it is now largely forgotten having been out of print for many decades.

Nicholson dedicated *Man and Literature* quite simply to:

> *The members of the W.E.A. at Millom, St. Bees and Whitehaven.*

The themes of the book are arguably more than a little-dated for 21st Century tastes: they were taken from Nicholson's late-1930s lectures to conferences of the Student Christian Movement at Swanwick, from which emerged in 1940 an article in the S.C.M.'s Journal, *Theology* [259] In this article, Nicholson highlighted Bernard

Shaw's alleged response to a reporter asking him which twelve men and women writers he'd choose to save if he were Noah preparing for another flood, to which Shaw had allegedly replied that he'd save none of them, but would let them all drown. This, Nicholson pointed out, was a grotesque example of the 'pre-war generation' of novelists who he claimed were wholly concerned with the relationship between Man and Society and totally indifferent to the individual relationship between a Man and his personal God.

Fortuitously, a letter from Nicholson to S.L. Bethell written on Boxing Day 1943, mainly about this particular book, has survived.[260] Nicholson had been suffering very badly indeed from the effects of influenza during the winter of 1943[261], but nonetheless expressed in his letter the hope that he would be able to meet up with 'SL' (as was his salutation) the following summer, presumably when the Bethell family paid their annual holiday visit from Bethell's Cardiff home to ancestral home ground in West Cumbria.

Nicholson mentions in the letter the various reviews of *Man and Literature* to date; that he had been pleased with the review in the *TLS*, because the reviewer had understood that which the book was not setting out to do, thereby avoiding some of the disgruntled misrepresentations of other reviewers, especially *The Listener* reviewer whom Nicholson suspected was *Stephen* (perhaps 'Spender').[262]

Nicholson goes on in the letter to express satisfaction that other reviews have to date been favourable:

particularly, *The Church Times* (for which Nicholson warmly thanks Bethell); *John O'London's Weekly*; and the *Catholic Herald,* even though Nicholson observed that the latter's reviewer had praised the book highly in a private letter to Nicholson, but had been rather more critical in the text of their published review.

Nicholson cited Galsworthy, H.G. Wells and Arnold Bennett as sharing this Shavian view of Man as an entirely social animal, where, Nicholson conjectured, if Man were to be placed alone behind a big and high brick wall, it wouldn't matter one jot to this faction as to what that Man got up to. He contrasted this group of authors with D.H. Lawrence particularly, to whom Man's spirituality was both omnipotent and omnipresent: to whom every moment in a Man's life was of supreme spiritual importance and to whom Man's individual morality rather than mere social expediency ought always and essentially to matter most. This commentary illuminates Nicholson's earlier decision to anthologise items of Lawrence's poetry as exemplars of modern 'Religious Verse': indeed, Nicholson confidently asserts in *Man and Literature* that:

> *No man of our time was more capable of comprehending the Christian doctrine than was Lawrence.*

Nicholson And Cowper

Nicholson's deep interest, beginning as a young adult, in the life and work of the 18th Century poet and hymn-writer William Cowper (1731-1800) is an essential component of Nicholson's *oeuvre,* but when this interest first emerged is not clear. Perhaps Nicholson's pre-Linford boyhood experiences of Methodist Millom and of its evangelical heritage, including the regular selection for services of worship of those many fine Newton and Cowper *Olney Hymns* first caught Nicholson's ear with their fine imagery, but this is pure speculation.

Prior to 1948, Nicholson's interest in Cowper was evident in his beautiful and sensitive early poem *The Tame Hare*, which was first published in Nicholson's 1948 sequel to his first-published collection *Five Rivers* - the critically unfavourably regarded *Rock Face.* The inspiration for the poem was possibly a very old (1784) published magazine article by Cowper:

Extract[263] From William Cowper's "Account of the Treatment of his Hares" - first printed in the Gentleman's Magazine, May 28th, 1784

Puss grew presently familiar, would leap into my lap, raise himself upon his hinderfeet, and bite the hair from my temples. He would suffer me to take him up, and to carry him about in my arms, and has more than once fallen fast asleep upon my knee. He

> *was ill three days, during which time I nursed him, kept him apart from his fellows, that they might not molest him, for, like many other wild animals, they persecute one of their kind that is sick, and by constant care, and by trying him with a variety of herbs, restored him to perfect health. No creature could be more grateful than my patient after his recovery; a sentiment which he most significantly expressed by licking my hand, first the back of it, then the palm, then between all the fingers, as if anxious to leave no part unsaluted; a ceremony which he never performed but once again upon a similar occasion…*

Cowper's own prose account was magnificently transmuted by Nicholson, in his poem, which began:-

> *She came to him in dreams - her ears*
> *Diddering like antennae, and her eyes*
> *Wide as dark flowers…*

Nicholson went on to publish a full-length literary biography of Cowper, in 1951, followed in 1960 by a short booklet commissioned by The British Council in their *Writers and their Work* Series[264] and in 1975 an Introduction to a Faber edition of Cowper's selected poems[265]. In 1951, Nicholson compiled a selection of Cowper's verse[266], published by Charles Wrey Gardiner's Grey Walls Press. Curiously, in a handwritten addendum to this book's listing in his thesis, Philip Gardner noted that it was 'not publicly released'. Yet second-hand copies of this book are still available, albeit exclusively in North America. Publication of this compilation, with an Introduction by Nicholson coincided with another publisher (John Lehmann)[267] launching Nicholson's biography of Cowper, so it may possibly have been a publisher's restrictive covenant (or other pressure) which gave his biography publisher sole UK rights to all publications of anything which Nicholson wrote at that time about Cowper, but no evidence to confirm or otherwise explain this has survived. C.W. Gardiner (1901-1981), although largely forgotten in the present day, was yet another important node in the connections of mid-twentieth-century literary networking. He was a book publisher and himself a poet and writer; he edited *Poetry Quarterly*, one of the leading poetry journals of the War years and of the 1950s. His extensive network of literary contacts included many of Nicholson's friends - for example, John Heath Stubbs, Alex Comfort and Kathleen Raine. His colourful and full life included three marriages and three now-forgotten published volumes of autobiography, to which he gave the last one the very apt and witty title of *The Answer to Life is No!* No papers relating to Gardiner survive in Nicholson's Rylands Collections, although Emory University Library in Atlanta, U.S.A. holds a collection of Gardiner's papers.[268]

Nicholson's particular interest in the work of Cowper is noted by Gardner in his thesis. Furthermore, though Gardner perhaps implies[269] that Nicholson's interest went rather beyond an affinity, into the realms of a close personal identification with this 18th Century poet. In particular, in discussing the reasons why the close friendship between Nicholson and Enrica Garnier had not progressed towards marriage, Gardner states that there were several reasons for this, some of them not known, but one of them, Gardner asserts, was certainly Nicholson's frail physical health.[270] - and that the same or similar difficulties had been encountered by Cowper.

Although Cowper throughout his life had revelled in the company of women he always drew fearfully back, almost in terror, from any of the usual ultimate intimacies. Nicholson himself speculates in his Cowper biography[271] that the sudden death of Cowper's mother when the young infant was just six years of age combined in at least equal measure with doubts about his (i.e., Cowper's, as Nicholson delicately put it, 'physical condition') led him to shy away from any suchlike intimacy. Nicholson speculates that Cowper thereafter was, at least subconsciously, seeking a mother-substitute, and cites Cowper's own description of his later close relationship with Mary Unwin as like mother and son as evidence, especially in view of the fact that Mary had been only seven years older than Cowper. Gardner's thesis does not discuss this additional 'mother substitute' dimension, but the general hints in Gardner's thesis of potential Cowper/Nicholson close similarities are fairly pronounced.

By 1960, in his Cowper booklet for The British Council, Nicholson had, most interestingly, by then changed his 'physical condition' allusion as above about Cowper to (Cowper's) 'mental condition', perhaps indicating that Nicholson himself no longer felt justified in perpetuating, even in a qualified way, the various speculations about Cowper which had circulated after his death, relating mainly to alleged abnormalities surrounding his physical gender and his physical sexual organs: speculation which had extended to Cowper having been described (without any sound evidence) as 'hermaphrodite'. Nicolson himself, in his 1951 full Cowper biography[272], had repeated these, albeit with some reservations:

> *...There have been suggestions also, based on merest hints, that he was, or suspected himself to be, a partial hermaphrodite.*

In a footnote, Nicholson pointed out that these suggestions were based entirely upon hearsay, but that something at least remotely of that ilk may have accounted for his (Cowper's) fear of marriage.

Dr Conrad Brunström of the National University of Ireland is a recent debunker of these speculative innuendos relating to Cowper's sexuality. He has been joined in this regard[273] by Neil Curry (poet, author, former friend of Nicholson and Editor for Faber and Faber of Nicholson's posthumous edition of Nicholson's *Collected Poems).*

Brunström[274] sets the scene succinctly:

> *It is the paradoxical intention of this paper to grapple firmly and yet obliquely with the issue of William Cowper's sexuality, searching not for an identity but rather for endless possibilities of identity. By refusing to settle for the notion that Cowper was either 'straight' or 'conventionally' queer/gay/molly/sodomitical, a far more radical challenge to heteronormativity presents itself when considering the life and legacy of this extraordinary and perplexing writer. Discussion of Cowper's sexuality has been limited and fragmentary to date, largely due to an ill-founded rumour of hermaphroditism, dating back to his early biographer Robert Southey...*

Brunström continues:

> *William Cowper loved women. He was incapable of living without women and all of the closest relationships of his life were with women. As one of his most important biographers, Charles Ryskamp, notes: 'For most of his life William associated with women every day - there were always one or more women hovering in the background, or sitting beside him in the parlours at Olney or Weston. His friendships were carefully non-sexual...*

Brunström points out that Cowper himself vehemently denounced sodomy, yet Cowper too renounced conventional heterosexuality; moreover, that Cowper, rather than demonstrating asexuality, could on occasions be positively sexy. And that Cowper's long and intense relationship with Mrs Unwin could not ever have become regarded as 'respectable' if Cowper had appeared to be a conventional heterosexual.

Similarly, Neil Curry observed:

> *Clearly [i.e., Cowper's] problem was an emotional one and I would tentatively suggest some degree of latent and unacknowledged homosexuality. I have noticed the number of times in his poems that he is angered by what he sees as 'effeminacy'. And this might explain why he was so attractive to women. It is not uncommon. One of my close friends, who is married to his gay partner, is nevertheless adored by almost every woman he meets*[275]*. And Cowper was adored, not only by Mrs Unwin, but by Lady Austen, and by his cousins Harriet and Theadora.*

Here, Curry prefers to apply the term *homosexuality* whereas Brunström avoids anything more specific than *queer*[276], but, if one applies all such terminology as fairly loose, relating merely to very variable positions on a wide sexuality spectrum, the differences are possibly largely semantic.

Nicholson's own affinity for - and identification with - William Cowper is plain. Far less clear, of course, is the extent if any to which Nicholson himself can be invested with any of Cowper's make-up and traits and preferences. As T.S. Eliot put it in another context, we have only '*hints and guesses*'.

Nicholson and Wordsworth (And Eliot)

Nicholson, in 1949, compiled a lengthy 'expert' commentary for a virtually forgotten book *Wordsworth: An Introduction and a Selection by Norman Nicholson*, published by a now defunct subsidiary of the firm of J.M. Dent Ltd., namely, Phoenix House which traded during c.1945 to 1965.[277] Other miscellaneous Wordsworth-related commentary featured in many items of Nicholson's broadcasting and journalism, and prominently in his poem *To the River Duddon*. In addition, Nicholson, at the age of seventy, was invited to appraise Wordsworth's achievements as a poet during the (1984) compilation of Melvyn Bragg's television arts documentary programme, *The South Bank Show.*

His broadcast comments about Wordsworth were unequivocal, but nonetheless very mixed: he asserted that Wordsworth had written some of the finest poetry in the English language, but much poetry which was second-rate too. Nicholson attributed this to the fact that Wordsworth had had excessive time on his hands, not being obliged to 'work' for his assured, prosperous, sinecure-funded living.

Many of Nicholson's views in 1984 seem to have changed little from some of those expressed in *To the River Duddon*, which had been written over forty years previously and which, in colloquial modernistic language, described Wordsworth somewhat defiantly as:

> *...a middle-aged Rydal landlord,*
> *With a doting sister and a pension on the civil list,*

Who left his verses gummed to your rocks like lichen,
The dry and yellow edges of a once-green spring...

- the whole implication of Nicholson's poem being fairly plainly that Wordsworth's *Duddon Sonnets* fell squarely within exactly-that category of the second-rate.

Nicholson had the acuity of critical perception to see both Wordsworth and Eliot not in the conventional critical wisdom as innately incompatible, but as fellow-revolutionary innovators and reformers of the poetic diction of their respective eras. In 1948, speaking primarily in praise of Eliot, Nicholson observed:

> *...It was not just that Mr Eliot had burst through the seams of a worn-out and shabby diction -this had been done before. Wordsworth had done the same thing for his generation by relating poetic diction to common speech. Moreover Wordsworth succeeded better than anyone before or since because he had a wonderful sense for those words which are so essential, so basic to the language and the emotions, that they scarcely change their significance from age to age. If you examine the poems like the Matthew and the Lucy series you will find that hardly a word he uses has become debased in meaning. Mr Eliot, however, related poetry not so much to common speech (though he made some experiments in that line in his dramatic works and monologues) but to that great commerce of language from which the modern reader draws his vocabulary - slang, journalism, literature and every other possible*

source. The result was that in these earlier poems he did not so much create a poetic diction as make it possible for other poets to create theirs[278]

Nicholson also wrote at some length about Wordsworth and his poetry about a year later for the then-popular magazine *Picture Post,* the main thrust of this article being the contrast between the younger Wordsworth at his literary finest and the elder Wordsworth's mostly lacklustre output. However, both in this magazine article and in his more scholarly Wordsworth compilation commentary Nicholson largely overlooks these later *dry and yellow edges of a once-green spring* and asserts, similarly to his previously published views, that without Wordsworth and without Wordsworth's unflagging faith in his own genius:

...poetry would have become dated and dead, a mere period piece like an antique chair. Again, he was practically the first English poet for 200 years to realise that poetry must not restrict itself to certain approved subjects, but must range over the whole of human knowledge and experience. In fact, he seems to almost have anticipated the problems of our world today[279] *when he says that "If the labours of Men of Science should ever create any material revolution in our condition....the Poet will sleep then no more than at present.*[280]

Nicholson further and specifically dismissed (most of) Wordsworth's later work in his 1949 book Introduction:

> *I do not wish to defend the older Wordsworth, but would say that, since he ceased to be a poet round about 1808, whatever happened to him later may be interesting to his biographers but has little to do with his poetry.*[281]

Nicholson, with very considerable insight, saw the achievements of both Wordsworth and Eliot as significant - and similar - as inspired and largely successful campaigns to 'purify the dialect of the tribe'. Over half a century later, the contemporary Eliot scholar, Prof. Jewel Spears Brooker has reflected upon the deeper similarities between the work of Wordsworth and Eliot as well as their strong (but superficial?) differences. This formed the topic of a lecture delivered by Brooker to the 2012 Little Gidding / T.S. Eliot Society Annual Festival, but not otherwise published. In this regard, Brooker notes an observation made by Coleridge that:

> *...historically distant and philosophically diverse men "whose characters at the first view appear widely dissimilar," can share deep similarities..*[282]

Brooker cites similarities in the style of reasoning of both poets and in their philosophy that Life tends to involve arriving back where one first started, but knowing it then for the first time; also in their approach to time and to Life's moments of epiphany which defy and transcend time itself.

Although not exactly pointing out such as the above specific Wordsworth-Eliot similarities, in his 1949 Introduction, Nicholson, (as well as pointing out that both poets had totally reformed and modernised worn-out poetic diction in general) saw further similarities in the background presence of Dante:

> *…Wordsworth admitted that his first pleasure in nature was purely animal ('Vivid the transport, vivid though not profound'), but he believed that later he grew into deeper communion. For my part I am ready to suspect that this first animal response to nature, however little understood at the time, was the most whole response he ever made. A sacrament does not require the intellectual co-operation of the recipient, but only that he should not set up any obstacle (and the greatest obstacle is self-consciousness) to the efficacy of grace…*[283]

10.5 Nicholson and H. G. Wells

In *WEC*[284] Nicholson mentions that he first read Wells's *Kipps* whilst still at school, and had even then been struck by the similarities, both in appearance, demeanour, and personality, between Kipps and his own father, Joseph Nicholson. Later (as also mentioned in *WEC*) whilst voraciously working through Linford Sanatorium's book library, Nicholson encountered all of H.G. Wells' works, along with those of similar ilk:

> *Wells, Bennett and Shaw spoke to me of the kind of society I had known before I came to Linford and they confirmed what I had already begun to think about it…..*[285]

Nicholson went on to devote a complete chapter of his (1943) *Man and Literature* book to Wells, placing him firmly in his 'Liberal Man' category, alongside, for example, Arnold Bennett. Later, in 1950, Nicholson published a full critical biography of Wells[286] but subsequently his Wells studies were not sustained, save that the *Encyclopaedia Britannica's*[287] entry on Wells was compiled by Nicholson (in fact this was Nicholson's sole contribution to this encyclopaedia).

10.6 Nicholson and The Brontes

In 1947, Nicholson wrote the Introduction to a classic edition of *Wuthering Heights*.[288] Little further detail survives about the context of this particular piece of work, but Nicholson launched straight into his Introduction as follows:

> *No artist is an accident, yet if we try to explain genius in terms of heredity and environment we are very likely to misunderstand it greatly. But when a parsonage of a remote Yorkshire village in the nineteenth century produces three sisters, all of them novelists, and two of them novelists of genius, then surely the circumstances of that parsonage are worth notice.*

Nicholson may well have had himself just as much as the Brontes in mind, as regards the futility of genetic explanations for human traits and gifts such as exceptional creativity. Similarly, Norman's opinion of Emily Bronte seems equally most applicable to his own self:

> *...It is really a poet's prose, as Wuthering Heights is a poet's novel. It takes us into a world far beyond the nineteenth century, far beyond Yorkshire, and in the end far beyond the ways and works of man; it takes us beyond particular time and place, beyond past and future, beyond civilisation and morality, into the infinite cosmos, as Emily Bronte saw it - the world where the rocks, and the stones, the light, the sun, the stars and the soul of man were all one. And beyond even this was the god of her faith; greater than all manifestations...*

Curiously, this was Nicholson's first and last foray into 'Bronte Studies'. Nonetheless, it is written in Nicholson's ever engaging style and contains some exceedingly original and perceptive comments, revealing many aspects of Nicholson himself as well as critical evaluations of Emily Bronte.

11

Nicholson's Topographical Prose

Norman Nicholson's topographical prose may be less-regarded in literary terms than was his poetry, but it provided him with a steady income over many years, and it thus cross-subsidised his preferred role in life: as a poet. Little detailed evidence survives in Nicholson's papers as to the proportion of his income which the topographical prose generated, but it was undoubtedly substantial.

It all began in 1948 when Robert Hale published, as part of their *Counties* Series of topographical or regional guide books a guide to Cumberland and Westmorland which was written by Nicholson.[289] Background evidence as to how this opportunity came about is not readily available, but Nicholson was to remain a prominent name upon Robert Hale's author list for almost all of his future prose works, which, over many years, deservedly achieved considerable popularity and commercial success.

Evaluation of Nicholson's topographical prose has become something of a stumbling block over the years for scholarly critics of his work. Gardner's thesis, and later book, excluded all of it from his specific remit. Cooper, in his Nicholson thesis, does not ring fence it quite to this extent (as he does Nicholson's plays and novels) but it remains very much in the background. In contrast, Neil Curry has challenged Gardner's approach, pointing out that golden nuggets of poetic diction and imagery are invariably embedded in most of Nicholson's topographical prose.

Arguably, critics who choose to ignore Nicholson's prose entirely, simply on the grounds that it is not his poetry, take a rather limited and blinkered view: does it really matter whether for example a striking or finely-wrought image appears in *Greater Lakeland* as opposed to *Sea to the West*?

As originally published, nearly half of *Cumberland and Westmorland* is devoted to the physical geography and geomorphology of the region and to its flora and fauna. Only then, in Part II, is (early) Man introduced into this landscape. From thence onwards, Nicholson seeks to explain how all these settlers impacted upon the area – how the characteristics and traditions both of *'the Mardale shepherd and the Workington miner'* were shaped. From the very outset, then, Nicholson considers his remit very much to include the land and people of the areas of the 'picturesque' lakes with all their high fells and scenic lakes but to include in equal measure areas such as the often-overlooked post-industrial fringe of West Cumbria.

Nicholson's coverage in this book of the region's current habitation and human inhabitants was relatively sparse: there was a single chapter on *The Lakes Today* followed by two longer final chapters devoted to *The Mining Scene* and to *The Mining Towns.* A large folded map of the area was glued into the inside back cover.

The *TLS*'s tradition of maintaining the anonymity of their book reviewers hid from public view that their review of the newly-published *Cumberland and Westmorland* had in fact been undertaken by Nicholson's close friend, Michael Roberts' widow, Janet.[290] Nonetheless, few other UK writers of the day would have posssessed Janet's affinity with this area. Nicholson's deep concern that the area must be rescued from the dangers of becoming a well-meaningly preserved but inevitably a decaying, tourist exhibit is astutely noted by the reviewer, as is Nicholson's rather Audenesque special interest in industry (the 'mines on the moor'). Janet commented upon the strength of Nicholson's attachment to the edgelands of West Cumbria. She observed, however, that other places on the eastern fringes of Cumberland and Westmorland, such as the town of Appleby, were hardly mentioned at all by Nicholson.

It is very apparent that this *TLS* review was alive to the fact that Nicholson's mental map of the area of Cumberland and Westmorland as a whole was, perhaps inevitably, constrained both by his Millom location and by his quite severe inability to travel to locations far away from his home base, many of which would have been inaccessible to him by any form of public transport. The fragility of Nicholson's health would also have ruled out any sustained or frequent travelling around this very remote and large region of the country, when the logistics may otherwise have permitted it. Nicholson's personal finances had probably improved somewhat, following the commercial success of *Five Rivers,* along with the beginnings of some income from jobbing journalism, but Nicholson's personal finances probably had a very long way to go to reach even the level of, say, any ordinary fit and employed young man in Millom, and probably remained reliant upon those of his parents. But this first topographical book perhaps represented the start of Nicholson's route towards financial independence – and indeed ultimately towards when he might contemplate marriage.

Nicholson's topographical works from the outset were not mere 'guidebooks'. As Janet Adam Smith observed, they served most effectively to enhance the understanding of the area both for visitors and even for residents who already knew parts of it well. Nicholson's book offered expert commentary about the area as it was perceived by an accomplished poet, and that insight was something rare and valuable and unique.

The dedicatee of Nicholson's first topographical book was his former Junior School Head Teacher at Holborn Hill School, Walter Wilson, whom Nicholson described in the dedication simply as his 'schoolmaster and friend'. In his autobiography, *WEC,* Nicholson devotes several pages to the reasons for his admiration and respect for Wilson.

Furthermore, Nicholson explained that, prior to teacher training, Wilson had taken a degree in Biology purely in order to deepen his understanding of Botany, a lifelong enthusiasm which he passed on to Nicholson, who came regularly to share with Wilson his many 'finds' of rare wild plants which he found growing within the Millom area.

The photographs of Cumbrian fells and landscapes contained in *Cumberland and Westmorland* have changed little in over sixty years, but one of the first book's illustrations unfortunately was a view of [291]Penrith Bus Station, full of (to present-day eyes) antiquated cars and motor coaches which were very clearly pre-war. *Cumberland and Westmorland* quite quickly went out of print. The production costs of a new edition in the same form were deemed by the publishers to be prohibitive, but, when popular demand for one grew, it was revamped in 1963 under the new title of *Portrait of the Lakes,* part of a new Robert Hale Publishers series of UK topographical books, which included works on Cornwall, on Devon and one of the Isle of Man. Essentially, the formula was the same but the original text was cut considerably in quantity and was partially rewritten, and re-arranged. The two chapters on the flora and fauna were dropped completely and the volume of illustrations cut by half, this time omitting the images of Penrith Bus Station.

The revised book was still dedicated to Walter Wilson, but Yvonne Nicholson's wife's motor car had widened her husband's travel opportunities immensely and she was then available readily to convey him '*to many parts of this district which otherwise I would have been unable to see'*, as Nicholson's comment on the 'acknowledgements' page expressed it.[292]

For Christmas 1963,'Nic' sent to his close friend George Every an inscribed copy of this, his latest topographical book.[293] Earlier (1955) Nicholson had brought out *The Lakers*[294] which was a Nicholson-edited anthology of the published experiences of others, who had been some of the first tourists to the Lake District. Amongst the generally favourable reviews of *The Lakers* was a perceptive and finely-wrought one by the Irish novelist Elizabeth Bowen (1899-1973), who admiringly remarked:

> *...(it) is more than a good book: I do not doubt that it will become a classic. Few of the many quotations the author gives exceed in energy and beauty, imagination and exactitude, his own.*

Sadly, the book was not destined to become a classic, despite it containing some fine examples of Nichoson's own prose. For just one of many glorious examples, Nicholson described how it can feel to contemplate from around Crummock the soaring slopes of Grassmoor and startlingly to experience a big shift-up of perceptual gearing, and a completely fresh perspective on simply 'being there':

> *...immediately the fellside comes into perspective and you feel the whole height and weight and mass of it hulking above you like a boot above a beetle....*

I would like to suggest that Nicholson's prose passages such as that one above are at least as worthy as his actual poetry: 'worthy' of both public enjoyment and of serious academic scrutiny. They are quite the equal of some of the best lines of his actual poetry, for example:

> *There stands the base and root of the living rock,*
> *Thirty thousand feet of solid Cumberland.*[295]

In 1977 Nicholson published another anthology, *The Lake District: An Anthology*[296] which was of broader scope than *The Lakers,* and contained selected passages by the usual sources such as Gilpin, Mrs Radcliffe, William and Dorothy Wordsworth, Coleridge and Ruskin but included alongside them far more modern examples of prose and poetry: examples from Nicholson himself, Margaret Cropper, from his friends Irvine Hunt, Melvyn Bragg, Graham Sutton and John Wyatt from his very fine book, *The Shining Levels*,[297] (which Nicholson once reviewed with immense enthusiasm in the *TLS*). Apart from showcasing some of Nicholson's own work and other fine pieces which Nicholson admired, the book reflects the very wide scope and considerable depth of his knowledge of his beloved area.

In 1991, four years after Nicholson's death, Irvine Hunt, whom Nicholson in his will had appointed his Literary Executor, edited *Norman Nicholson's Lakeland: A Prose Anthology*[298] which presented a further selection from Nicholson's complete topographical prose *oeuvre.*

This included considerable material from Nicholson's final topographical prose work *Greater Lakeland*[299] which had been published in 1969 and reprinted twice, in 1970 and 1975, with a paperback edition published in 1996, indicating some commercial success both for Nicholson the author and for his publishers (Robert Hale).

The concluding words of *Greater Lakeland* provide yet another example of Nicholson's prose at its finest, and are well worth repeating here, both to illustrate his mastery of words and his penetrating insight into the whole of the Cumbria region:

> *...Perhaps Greater Lakeland could be defined as the country where the Lake fells are in sight. But the unity is greater than that. It comes from the rock, from the shape of the land, from its history, and from the stock and breeding of its people. It embraces places which the visitor to the Lakes may not want to see and aspects of life and society which he comes here to forget. But it is no good trying to forget them. Greater Lakeland does not just mean Derwentwater, Blea Tarn and the Wasdale Screes: it also means Windscale Atomic Station, the Marchon chemical factory at Whitehaven, Workington Steelworks, Barrow Docks and Carlisle Railway Depot; wharves, warehouses, bus-stops and parking-places; schools, adult-education centres, the county libraries; churches, chapels, Sunday schools, cinemas and dance-halls; sports fields, allotments and cemeteries; the new housing estates and the old, shabby Victorian terraces; hardware stores, chemists',*

> *fish-and chip shops, pubs and coffee-bars; the dairy herds, turnip fields and pig-sties of a thousand lowland farms; one cathedral, one teachers' training college, one Polaris-submarine ship-building yard—in fact, all that goes to the life and death of the people of the old kingdom and the new county of Cumbria. Forget all this, and what all the rest of the country calls 'Lakeland' will turn moribund, dying slowly from the edges inwards, to become in the end little more than a beautiful, embalmed corpse in a rotting coffin.*

Nicholson's observations of nearly forty-five years past have since proved to have been farsighted and accurate - essentially prophetic: gone forever are such industries and economic activities as Whitehaven's various coal mines and its giant Marchon chemical factory; Workington's extensive steelworks and Carlisle's vast marshalling yard have disappeared too. Perhaps the rot, so feared by Nicholson, set in, and continues apace.

'Windscale Atomic Station' is now re-badged as 'Sellafield' and (fortunately for the economic wellbeing of West Cumbria) is by far the area's biggest direct and indirect employer. Sellafield is now West Cumbria's only surviving (and therefore ever-vulnerable) economic lifeline, although the functions of that site have changed very considerably since its first construction. It is interesting to trace the attitudes towards the 'Atomic Station' which Nicholson expressed over the years in his topographical prose, and to contrast these largely ambivalent and neutral opinions with those evident in his very emotive protest poem *Windscale,* where:

...children suffocate in God's fresh air.

When Nicholson wrote *Cumberland and Westmorland* in 1948, this remote spot where the rivers Ehen and Calder flow into the sea had been a wartime munitions factory which Nicholson fairly neutrally noted was:

...soon to become an atomic power plant...

Nicholson did however add an apprehensive comment that he feared that wholesale factory development might be out of place in such a rural area anticipating in a sense his view in his later anti-nuclear poem, *Windscale,* which begins by observing with obvious distaste (even disgust) that:

The toadstool towers infest the shore...

By the early 1960s, and when *Portrait of the Lakes* was published, in spite of Nicholson having lived through the effects of that 1957 Windscale reactor fire and catastrophic radiation pollution, and in spite of his earlier indignant *Windscale* protest poem (a poem which has become almost the anthem of the anti-nuclear lobby) Norman maintained a circumspect yet balanced attitude towards the whole nuclear industry. For example, he wrote:

...I am not one who thinks that the splitting of the atom is likely to be a boon to mankind, but Sellafield (which

is how Cumberland people always refer to the atomic station) has played a great part in the west coast revival. It has given new jobs to the men of the worked-out mining towns; it offers careers for local boys with technical and scientific training; and it has produced our most impressive industrial architecture since the blast-furnaces.

Above all, it has given the once-isolated West Cumbrians a sense of being in the front line of the twentieth century. We have already paid for this dubious honour by pouring our milk down the drains during the radioactive leak of a few years ago; we may pay at a higher price in the future. But, at present, Sellafield helps to keep more than just the Geiger counters ticking...

Note the apprehension about building development has turned to admiration of it now as *impressive industrial architecture* and Nicholson's rather misogynistic assumptions that only males become scientists.

This rather scrupulous and measured even-handedness spills over into *Greater Lakeland*, where, commenting upon the coastal village of Seascale, Nicholson wrote:

The world's first atomic-power station was built just two miles away at Sellafield, and Seascale jumped forward a whole half century in five years. A new, expensive housing estate has mushroomed up between the old village and Gosforth, and nearly all the habitable cottages and country houses within nine or ten miles have been bought up by scientists from Calder Hall. Seascale and district now holds the greatest concentration of the highly educated that Greater Lakeland has ever known, while the proportion of B.Scs. per housing square foot must be one of the highest in England.

All this is helping to change West Cumberland society, and its effects can be seen in the music and dramatic societies, in the support given to Rosehill Theatre[300]*, and even in the manners of the children at the local schools.*

Yet, in spite of all the new money and the new faces, Calder Hall darkens the landscape like a threat. It is not that the buildings themselves are ugly, except for the clutter of car parks and dumps and wire-netting at the periphery. The original towers—now, apparently, already out of date—were slim and elegant, and the new cooling towers, though less pleasing in shape, often turn the coast into a Chinese watercolour with their twisting wraiths of mist. [301]*But when there was an atomic leak at the plant in the late fifties, and we, in Millom, had to pour our milk down the drains, we felt as if we were waiting for lightning to strike from a clear sky.*

There was no recognisable sign of danger, but the air seemed electric. The atom, in fact, is not a comfortable neighbour. Yet atomic fission is now a fact that has to be faced, and at Calder Hall they are facing it and trying to make the best of it. If the splitting of the atom does not

> *put an end to the world, Calder Hall may help to turn it from a menace to a hope.*

But Nicholson could not resist playfully repeating some of the local myths about the place (allied, characteristically nonetheless to his usual spirit of geographical and topographical didacticism):-

> *Immediately out of Seascale you run beside the golf-course, with Calder Hall*[302] *like a grotesque hazard for the sliced drive. This is the country of the new science-fiction folklore: how a Lakeland terrier swam across a certain beck and came out of the water completely hairless; and how scientists, having cooked their golf-balls, go round the course in the dark with the aid of a Geiger-counter. The atomic station itself is built near the outlet of the River Calder, where it divides into a gravelly delta.*

12

Nicholson's Autobiographical Prose

Nicholson's main autobiographical prose works were *Provincial Pleasures*, (1959), which was a thinly-fictionalised account of a year in the life of 1950s Millom as experienced by Nicholson as narrator, and of course *WEC*, his autobiography covering his formative years from early childhood until his late-teens which he published much later, in 1975. Following its publication as a book, it was serialised in the local newspaper serving Millom and surrounding areas.

Provincial Pleasures resulted in considerable speculation amongst Millom's inhabitants about exactly who the 'fictional' characters had been based-upon. This even led to *The Daily Mail* national newspaper despatching two reporters to Millom in the hope of tracking-down some alleged subjects of the book who were outraged at being 'fictionalised' by Nicholson: but they failed to come back with any good story.[303]

In 1954, Dylan Thomas's *Under Milk Wood* had been

broadcast by BBC Radio to some considerable public acclaim, and it is almost certain that Nicholson was very familiar with this play. The similarities between *Provincial Pleasures* and *Under Milk Wood* are fairly plain, although the *genre* differs, and *Provincial Pleasures* is in a more conventional illustrated book form, and not a 'play for voices' as *Under Milk Wood* had been conceived. Nicholson rather mundanely named Millom his usual 'Odborough' unlike Thomas's ingenious and mischievous comic 'Llareggub' ('bugger all' spelled backwards). And Nicholson's work, although entertainingly-written, rather lacks the bawdy, chaotic sustained comic exuberance of the Thomas play: as if Nicholson's purpose had been to celebrate day to day life in a small provincial town[304], whereas Thomas's was to use his verbal virtuosity and comic wit to provide 'pure' entertainment (which necessarily incorporated plenty of sex).

13

Nicholson's Poetry

13.1 An Introduction

Whilst his topographical books, together with prolific journalism, provided him with his main income,[305] as has often been said within this book, Nicholson considered himself primarily to be a poet, and is so described, with simplicity yet great dignity, on his own tombstone. He is on record as saying emphatically that it was for his poetry he would wish to be remembered, but at the same time he firmly declined to single out any particular poems in this regard.[306]

Although very much in his own, idiosyncratic style, Nicholson's poetry retained at least some roots in the new realism and the prevailing general climate of modernism of the 1930s and 1940s. But, Nicholson himself, perhaps a little playfully, asserted that he was a modern, as opposed to a modernist poet.[307] His fundamental preference was for poetry to be intelligible, rather than obscure: some of the reasons behind this purpose have already been touched upon. Perhaps inescapably, though, he was influenced by the work of contemporary poets, for example, Hopkins, Auden and many others, but overwhelmingly by T.S. Eliot.

Nicholson himself fully recognised and bemoaned the inevitable and very considerable difficulties entailed in finding his own poetic 'voice', particularly as regards separating his own voice from that of T.S. Eliot[308], and, of course, from the pervasive influence of Wordsworth. In one of his interviews for local radio, for example, he quoted Kathleen Raine as once having observed that Norman Nicholson could produce quite the best lines which T.S. Eliot did not himself happen to have written. Nicholson's own poetic *oeuvre* does tend to defy classification: he was decidedly not in any very meaningful way simply another poet of the Georgian School, although he has been labelled as such, for example, by Gifford[309].

Gifford is one comparatively recent critic who has been fairly dismissive of Nicholson's work. He has described it as 'pretentiously naive', 'whimsical', and 'wistful', displaying, he alleges, an uncritical regard for the pastoral, coupled simplistically with stereotypical distaste for the urban landscape[310]. The poetry of Ted Hughes is, in contrast, generally acclaimed by Gifford.

However, there is a case that Gifford's views run counter to the reality. Nicholson had originally been deeply influenced by the 'pylon poets' of the 1930s; he regarded and celebrated the whole of Creation as an organic, dynamic, God-made, unique and integrated system, irrespective of whether it happened to be rural or urban, biological, geological or sociological. Gifford's particular criticisms therefore do not stand up to close scrutiny in this context.

Nicholson was by no means in awe of Ted Hughes's poetry, once cautiously describing it to a visiting journalist as 'fine, if not always clear.'[311] Nicholson would probably have robustly defended himself against such as Gifford's accusations of whimsy and being compared unfavourably as a poet with Ted Hughes. In a 1976 local radio interview Nicholson was directly invited to comment upon the criticism that his outlook was strictly local and 'provincial' in the sense of limited and confined. He responded in his characteristically robust manner, emphasising that most of his poetic subjects, albeit often things directly encountered within his local patch, had nonetheless a far more general – even universal - significance, and he cited wanton and greedy exploitation of the world's natural resources and the perils of Man's experimentation with nuclear energy and atomic bombs as prime examples. These concerns of course have now become very topical 'green' and environmental topics so many decades later.

Nicholson once, much earlier, was quite savagely criticised as a poet by fellow-poet George Barker (1913-1991) in a review in a well-respected literary magazine[312] of Nicholson's (then) newly published poetry collection, *The Pot Geranium*[313] Deploying considerable and derogatory sarcasm, Barker declared his exasperation with Nicholson's typical subject-matter, deriding Nicholson's poems about places and objects as mere *'catalogues'* hardly worthy of the description 'poetry'. In a closing flourish

Barker conceded that Nicholson had included just a few 'proper' poems too, efforts which might bring Nicholson's stature as a poet up to the level of around Wordsworth's heart, as opposed to Nicholson's usual place, looking at Wordsworth's knees.

This scathing and rather venomous and polemical review prompted Anne Ridler to write a letter of protest[314] to the magazine's editor, John Lehmann in which she said she would not expect such a *'Dionysiac'*[315] poet as Barker ever to appreciate one like Nicholson, but perhaps the Editor should print such as this under the far more appropriate heading of 'Unfair Comment'. Lehmann, the embarrassed Editor, simply published the protest letter without further comment, but is said privately to have deeply regretted the whole incident, saying that, had he known about Barker's unusual antipathy towards Nicholson, he would never have invited the review, but that when it came, it had been too late to strike it out.

However, Barker's comments may not have been all that they seemed. A leading UK English Professor has commented about them:

> *I know that review, which is re-printed in Barker's Collected Essays (1970). But I think that you have misread it. There is no "vehement dislike" there. It reads to me (who knew GB well), to have been written in a spirit of elaborate teasing. Barker very often teased those he loved and respected. He loved and respected David Gascoyne, whom he then called "the most boring man in*

Europe". Ridler, a much more literal-minded soul, would I think not have understood this.[316]

There was certainly little possibility of any 'elaborate teasing' in the letter which the distinguished historian and writer A.L. Rowse (1903-1997) was moved to write to Nicholson, who, perhaps uncharacteristically, allowed it to survive within his archives[317]. Rowse clearly took great offence at Nicholson's review of some of his poetry in the *Church Times* and Nicholson probably kept it as a curiosity, for reason of the arrogance and unpleasantness of its content.

Nicholson's style of poetry does tend both to impede and rather to defy labelling and conventional classification. Indeed, (in most part) it has been his fellow poets acting as critics as opposed to non-poet critics who have spotted and celebrated Nicholson's considerable technical accomplishment. For example, the Liverpool academic and poet, Matt Simpson (1936-2009) declared that Nicholson was *'among the most gifted poets of his century...... as accomplished as and certainly less limited in outlook than Larkin'*[318], and, in the same article, Simpson joined Neil Curry in commenting upon the typically patronising (although probably well-intentioned) faint and carefully qualified praise deployed in Nicholson's (1987) *Times* obituary, that he had been *'the most gifted English, Christian, Provincial poet of his century*'[319].

But in total contrast to such positive commentary, there must be considered the hugely disparaging treatment of Nicholson at the hands of the influential Cambridge critic F.R. Leavis and his wife, Queenie, (Q.D.) in their literary magazine *Scrutiny*. Both of the Leavises were clearly very unimpressed indeed with Nicholson's early work[320], as they were with that of those of contemporaries of similar (Christian) outlook, such as the work of George Every and that of the Shakespearian scholar, Samuel Leslie Bethell[321]. One might conclude that certain *ad hominem* and prejudiced vendettas were being pursued by both of the Leavises. For example, the personal religious faith of all these individuals was derided by the Leavises at every possible opportunity. Similarly, they wrote sneeringly about Nicholson's and Every's connections with non-University 'extension' or even Workers' Educational Association audiences.[322]

Despite Nicholson himself being one of their most prolific book reviewers, the *Times Literary Supplement (TLS)* over the years seems amply to have justified Nicholson's own rather despairing grumble that he had been almost totally neglected as a poet[323]. In fact the website of the *TLS* incorporates a voluminous and highly detailed chronological survey of the whole body of Twentieth Century English Literature, but it never once mentions Norman Nicholson's input to any of it, nor any of his works as having contributed to it. It is as if a band of indifferent and blinkered cartographers had simply left Nicholson and all his works off the literary map. For further sad example, very few English Literature academics, especially within any universities outside Britain seem ever to have heard of Nicholson.[324]

Similarly, and even within the UK, during the 1980s the Open University ran an advanced undergraduate Arts Faculty course unit entitled *Twentieth Century Poetry*. This considered extensively works by Eliot, Yeats, Hardy, Larkin and even Betjeman in very considerable detail, but did not discuss Norman Nicholson.

During the 1940s, Nicholson had found himself elevated to the select band of Faber Poets. Perhaps a footracing metaphor is appropriate here: he had certainly moved up the field, well into the pack of the leading runners, but, as things were to turn out, he failed conspicuously to remain there when it came to the closing laps of the race.

What happened?

One explanation may be that, as the Faber poets of the 1940s raced on into the 50s and 60s, newer, fresher and mostly younger, contenders had moved up to join this pack of front-runners: these being contenders such as Philip Larkin and Ted Hughes.

Nicholson probably felt (perhaps with good reason) that he was being rather unjustifiably and unfairly elbowed-out, or, to mix metaphors, eclipsed by these newcomers. They were in many respects, even at their best, rather less accomplished, but far more fashionable than he, and many were far better placed as regards their home locations and visibility to critics. Even Nicholson's (slightly older) contemporary, the poet and writer John Betjeman, for whose works Nicholson seems to have had only limited admiration, was rapidly becoming a famous TV and radio personality: in fact, a 'national treasure'. In 1969, Betjeman received the huge honour of a Knighthood. In stark contrast, it was not until 1981 that Nicholson was awarded a far humbler O.B.E., and, in 1972, it was Betjeman and not Nicholson whom the Queen appointed Poet Laureate[325].

In similar demeaning fashion the satirical weekly magazine, *Private Eye*, in 1981, speculated upon who might become the then-ailing Sir John Betjeman's successor as Poet Laureate. Both Basil Bunting and Norman Nicholson were discussed by the *Eye* correspondent as possible outside candidates, but both were totally ruled out mainly by reason of their remoteness from the Metropolis / Home Counties. And, in pursuance of its long and proud tradition of never allowing the *Eye's* accuracy to spoil a potentially amusing and salacious story, the magazine's anonymous correspondent informed readers that the fiercely Northumbrian Bunting lived in Cumbria[326], and described him as being aged ninety-four (in reality, he was then 'only' eighty-one years old).

The correspondent went on in the same article to describe Nicholson as a generously-whiskered, smock-clad peasant;[327] a hangover from the Victorian era and an inhabitant of a remote backwater no-one had ever even heard of. Ridiculous and untrue, but perhaps illustrative of the price Nicholson had to pay for choosing to operate very much as a provincial poet and for daring to depart stylistically from conventional, fashionable poetry.

As early as in 1947, the prominent American poet, Kenneth Rexroth (1905-82), had written to Nicholson about an anthology he was editing, saying in passing that he personally regarded Nicholson as one of the ten most vital poets aged under forty in Britain[328]. In the early 1940s, too, in a letter to Nicholson the English poet, David Gascoyne (1916-2001) copiously praised Nicholson's work.[329]

Nicholson might be evaluated as in general having failed to build upon his considerable early promise. For example, his 1948 sequel to *Five Rivers*, *Rock Face*, proved somewhat pedestrian, and rather a damp squib. It was not until 1954, with his next collection, *The Pot Geranium,* that Nicholson was able to get back to any significant level of critical acclaim. But, following *The Pot Geranium*, Nicholson (for reasons discussed in an earlier chapter) withdrew himself from the poetical scene, during a fallow period that was to last for eighteen years. He returned, in 1972, aged 58, and changed considerably in thematic direction with the appropriately-titled *A Local Habitation*. This collection became another Poetry Book Society Choice. His last poetry collection was published in 1981 and bore the title *Sea to the West*.

Nicholson's protracted absence from the world of published poetry probably contributed significantly to this tendency for his work to have been placed by critics as well outside the First Division and its subject-matter was indeed quite often, but mistakenly, disregarded by many as being rather simplistic, tiresomely bucolic, overly-provincial, and merely descriptive.

Nicholson's personal, Christian religious faith suffuses the early parts of his *oeuvre*. But, in his later years, when interviewed by BBC local radio, Nicholson himself expressed regret that religious themes had, in his opinion and with the considerable benefit of hindsight, featured unduly prominently and too dogmatically in his earlier work, to its overall detriment. He recounted his oft-repeated explanation that his literary awakening had been the result of encountering the work of T.S. Eliot, together with his burgeoning interest in the natural world around him – its geology and flora and fauna, for example. The combination of these events (with, one might conjecture, his carefully shrouded love life as the catalyst) had led to his regaining a personal religious faith, and all of this combined and concentrated mental fervour had exploded from him, in torrents of creativity and thus poetry.

It seems that Nicholson was anxious to avoid any public attribution of this literary flowering to any experiences arising from his personal relationships, in particular with his longstanding liaison with Enrica Garnier, during the 1940s. Little direct evidence of this relationship has survived as a result of Nicholson's destruction of his archives, but it would be somewhat odd if this deeply felt relationship had not been a significant factor in this regard. For example, a few of his earlier poems, in *Five Rivers,* point to a very considerable affection on his part and furthermore point fairly plainly and assuredly, albeit with some untypically hyperbolic imagery, to rather intense personal passion:

...September sun as hot as a kiss of parting,
autumn songs of the chiffchaff and the chaffinch,
The herald moth like a withered leaf, the blue
rings of bilberries on the tiny lobes of the leaves.

...the fantastic
Spring of love in the blood, the brutal wooing of God.

(From September in Shropshire)

and

...In the blue dusk of the empty carriage
There is no more here nor there,
No more you nor me.
Green like a burning apple
The signal hangs in the pines beside the shore
And shines All Clear.
(From Coastal Journey)

The sense of strong attachment, between 'you' and 'me' intertwines in the above example with the religious and the natural and other imagery to form a hybrid kind of 'Love' poetry, which connects, subsumes and affirms Nicholson's intense love for another human being with both his love of God and of all of Creation and Nature. Nicholson here may be perceiving human love as a hint of God's love of Man, and as an integral and inevitable and worthy part of the same cycle of Life itself.

13. 2 Nicholson's Poetry: A Tentative Reappraisal

Between Nicholson's early and late poetry there is, arguably, little indication of any particular growth or developmental process, or, in modern parlance, there is no discernible learning curve. *Five Rivers* contains some (albeit in part they are flawed) highly accomplished poems, especially from a relative novice and newcomer. In particular, the title poem stands out in this regard, as does equally his irreverent swipe at Wordsworth, in the form of his fine poem *To the River Duddon*.

The title poem itself, *Five Rivers,* is an impressionistic verse description of a journey through particular South West Cumbrian coastal fringe areas, inspired by Nicholson's many journeys up and down the West Cumbrian branch railway line which connects Millom, in the far south, with the seaport of Whitehaven. The line continues to Carlisle, in the far north of the county, but ceases to hug the coast once it passes Workington. At Maryport, this branch line shoots away from the coast, across the adjacent plain towards Carlisle, where it ends at the main line Carlisle Citadel rail station.

Unlike many others, this branch line remains in passenger service to the present day: it is possible[330] therefore to experience today the same journey undertaken by the young Nicholson over seventy years ago. But, one might speculate, how differently might someone who was a total stranger to the area perceive the poem *Five Rivers,* which after all, is essentially poetry of place? To a native Cumbrian, familiar with, attuned to and regularly experiencing the places described, Nicholson's fresh viewpoints might evoke and delightfully enhance an individual's pre-existing and personal mental images, but, otherwise, is mere description, however original and accomplished, really sufficient to make for fine poetry? In the same regard, during the course of researching this book the following comment was made by a Philip Larkin enthusiast. It is otherwise unpublished commentary, but so very apt in this particular context that I make no apologies for repeating it in full, here:

> *....Millom is central to (Nicholson's) work. The town was, so to speak, his Muse, but it also, I agree, limited his audience. A friend of mine, from Millom, wonders how anybody outside the town can appreciate a lot of the poetry, and I think this is why Larkin discriminated (ie left Nicholson out of his Modern Verse compilation – as discussed later in this Chapter) - not because Nicholson couldn't "entertain," but because his appeal could be felt only by a minority, even if he was writing about "universal" issues through a "local" frame. His work is so specific to the place. Going back to Larkin, his poems would begin with place names and such like, yet with each draft he would gradually ease these out, allowing the reader to associate their own sense of place, person, and what not. If you look at a poem like 'Millom Old Quarry' almost every angle of town, right down to street names, is reflected. It is a fascinating, wonderful piece, but his dedication to Millom I feel did preclude wider appreciation.....*[331]

Nicholson would of course have urged us, his audience, closely to read and take full and considered heed of all of his words, but he recognised acutely that the reader is merely viewing words on a page, just as a person looking at a landscape or a 'view' merely forms a unique, personal and entirely subjective construct of that place in their own brain.

But, to return to the original *Five Rivers* poem, in one sense it presents a litany of river and place names, Nicholson having chosen to emphasise the former, both on the page *and* indirectly in the viewer's perception, in unusual and striking CAPITAL letters. John Betjeman (1906-1984) immediately comes to mind as having adopted similar treatment of everyday names and familiar places, so very typical and distinctive that it has been parodied playfully but with great effect by Alan Bennett:

Bolding Vedas! Shanks New Nisa!
Trusty Lichfield swirls it down
To filter beds on Ruislip Marshes
From my lav in Kentish Town

And, in comparison, a little trickle from the actual source waters, this being by Betjeman himself:

From the geyser ventilators
Autumn winds are blowing down
On a thousand business women
Having baths in Camden Town

Waste pipes chuckle into runnels,
Steam's escaping here and there,
Morning trains through Camden cutting
Shake the Crescent and the Square.

But Nicholson ranged a lot wider than Betjeman in quickly moving on stylistically from the poem *Five Rivers,* In an uncharacteristically waspish aside, Nicholson once even commented during a broadcast on the BBC Home Service:[332]

> *John Betjeman can write of the later developments of rail travel with the kind of sentiment which is usually kept for stage coaches on Christmas cards:*
>
> *When melancholy autumn comes to Wembley*
> *And electric trains are lighted after tea*
> *The poplars near the Stadium are trembly*
> *With their tap and tap and whispering to me…*

Betjeman's poetry collection, *A Few Late Chrysanthemums*, which contained the above poem 'came out' in 1954, coming into flower concurrently with Nicholson's own appropriately titled collection, *The Pot Geranium.* Although little or no further hard evidence of Nicholson's rating of Betjeman as a poet survives, one might well speculate that Nicholson felt himself unjustifiably in the shadow of this urbane, well-connected, upper middle class, arguably inferior, yet far more popular fellow poet.

Nicholson in his lifetime would, perhaps mercifully, never have been aware of Betjeman's own, somewhat disparaging dismissal of Nicholson's poetical skill.[333] This relates to a letter of 24 November 1944 to Geoffrey Handley Taylor (1920-2005) in which Betjeman wrote:

> *Norman Nicholson is an untechniqued poet. Marie Stopes is not. I become swamped with verse nowadays as these silly fools like to see themselves in the Daily Herald [see comments re Betjeman's column therein below]but the Daily Herald doesn't.*[334]

However, this private, somewhat catty and throwaway remark perhaps needs to be interpreted in context, as probably ill-considered hubris and certainly with much caution. Marie Stopes may have excelled in the field of birth control, but not in any lasting way as events turned out, as a poet. Betjeman's remark was a response to Nicholson's very first collection of poetry, *Five Rivers,* so, although it may not have been completely to his personal taste, subsequent Nicholson poetry may well have been more so, and probably resulted in a revision of this initial opinion. This would explain why Betjeman having decades later been appointed Poet Laureate himself recommended Nicholson for the award of the 1977 Queen's Gold Medal for Poetry, Betjeman participated supportively at the Gold Medal award ceremony by H.M. The Queen at Buckingham Palace and it was Betjeman who warmly heaped hospitality on Nicholson and his wife immediately after that event.

But, to return to 1944, Betjeman at that time wrote a regular weekly 'Books' column for *The Daily Herald*, in which he once reviewed Nicholson's newly-published first volume of poetry, *Five Rivers.* It was a somewhat mixed review, but certainly not unfavourable: Betjeman did indeed criticize aspects of Nicholson's technique, along with his alleged echoings of T.S. Eliot, but Betjeman stated emphatically that, nonetheless, Nicholson was *a real poet,* and that:-

> *...Only a poet could have described lichen on rock as 'the dry and yellow edges of a once-green spring.' It is for a hundred minute observations of nature like this that I am grateful to Mr. Nicholson.*[335]

Nicholson, many years later, experienced deep hurt when Philip Larkin decided not to include any of Nicholson's work in the (1973) *Oxford Book of Twentieth Century English Verse,* for which Larkin was Editor. Nicholson's indignant correspondence with Larkin on the matter survives in the Rylands Library.[336] Larkin had sought to justify the omission to Nicholson by pointing out that Nicholson's collection *A Local Habitation* (1972) had not been published by the time the *Oxford Book* went to print, in 1971, and that its primary function was to entertain its readers, and not necessarily to include examples of (technically) 'good' poetry. But these were somewhat lame excuses, implying that none of the poems in *Five Rivers* (1944) and *The Pot Geranium* (1954) had been considered worthy of inclusion by Larkin,

Larkin's rebuff must have been particularly hurtful to Nicholson, for, in 1955, Nicholson had been one of the few active donors ('subscribers' as they were then called) to Larkin's independently-published poetry collection *The Less Deceived* in acknowledgement of which Nicholson had earned a mention by name in the list of subscribers included in the back of the printed book. But this goodwill was not at all reciprocated by Larkin, who was moved to mention it in a private letter to his companion Monica Jones:

> *....About Norman N. - well, I don't care for him, I must admit, from what I know. I find his poetry rather 'smart', & his regionalism & Christianity I'd sooner infer than have crammed down my throat. Still, I'm very glad to have his six bob*[337] *& his name in the back......*[338]

Thus, the seeds of Larkin's antipathy towards Nicholson were planted many years before Larkin edited the *Oxford Book*. However, Larkin's disdain for Nicholson may have been somewhat more nuanced - even ambiguous - for in 1979 Larkin mentioned in a letter to his pal, Kingsley Amis that he and Monica had visited the Lake District and that their itinerary *trotting round the Lake District* (as he called it) had included *Norman Nicholson country at Millom.*[339] It is a fact that few if any visitors to the Lake District ever find themselves passing though or even close by the town of Millom (it is located absolutely at the far end of the 'edgeland', not on the route to any other place), so it is probably safe to infer that Larkin made a conscious and deliberate detour in order to inspect Nicholson's home town. Larkin tantalisingly provided no further details of his Millom foray, but it is probably entirely safe to infer that Larkin decided not even to entertain the thought of making any form of social call upon Nicholson at St. George's Terrace: Larkin and Monica may even have sneaked surreptitiously past Nicholson's big ground floor front window at Number 14, but we shall probably never know. [340]

It has already been mentioned (Chapter 13.1 above) that a totally-disparaging stance towards Nicholson and George Every and S.L. Bethell - was adopted by F.R. Leavis and by his wife, Queenie. F.R., In particular, both penned scathing personal attacks on Nicholson and on Every. F.R. Leavis seemed bent on ridiculing Nicholson's non-university education and the involvements of both Every and Nicholson in lecturing to non-university audiences. A brief snippet may illustrate the sheer disdain and vindictive tone of such remarks which evidently extended even to Charles Williams:

> *One might, after looking through the book, start by asking why Mr Every has devoted so much time to poetry, and to creative literature in general, since (I hope I may be forgiven for saying) he shows no compelling interest in it, and no aptitude for its study...*
>
> *...Of his own discovery and fostering Mr Every offers us, as poet and intellectual of established standing (we are*

> *to assume), Mr Norman Nicholson a writer in whom, I am bound to say, I can see no vestige of any gift, but only intentions and pretensions that have gathered assurance from assiduous encouragement and from the sense of swimming, shoal-supported, with the tide. But then, I can see no reason for being interested in Charles Williams, whom we are offered as a major power, and Mr Nicholson's inspirer...*[341]

An American edition of *Five Rivers* was published in 1945[342] and the collection came up, along with recent efforts by many other contemporary poets, for inspection and critical comment by Robert Lowell. Clearly Lowell was, like F.R. Leavis, a demanding critic who did not at all mince his words, or temper his appraisals, and, characteristically, Lowell began:

> *The eighteen books reviewed here can be roughly divided into three categories: the hopelessly untalented, the unsuccessful, and the realized. Such a classification is convenient but not entirely accurate. The unsuccessful range from poems by men of just a little ability who probably are doing about the best they can to botched poems of considerable promise. The good books are of very unequal distinction, and all include much that is worthless. They would have been much stronger if they had been cut in half, for good poetry is rare and no one writes often at even his second best. The hopelessly bad books need not be analysed. I have nothing to say about the absurd*

> *phony-Lindsay clatter of Mr Alan Baer Rothenberg, the ungrammatical pilfering of Mr George J. Cox, the slick and sounding oratory of Mr Carl Carmer or the harmless devotions of Mr Loyd Haberly. A few quotations would ruin these writers more effectively than any criticism...*[343]

Even Cecil Day-Lewis, who became Poet Laureate in 1968, became the recipient of the rather terrifying flamethrower that amounted to Lowell's critical scrutiny:

> *Mr C. Day Lewis is a man of energy and sensibility who apparently tosses off verses to amuse himself. He has neither improved nor deteriorated with the years. So careless are his rhymes, rhythms and tropes, that one suspects that the two volumes included in Short Is the Time were written at one sitting. He is verbal without craftsmanship; abstract without profundity. His romanticism has dash and no weight...*[344]

But, quite unlike Leavis in Cambridge, UK, Lowell, in contrast to his rather scornful dismissal of Day Lewis's latest efforts, placed the beginner-poet Norman Nicholson in his 'pretty good (at least in parts)' category:

> *Mr Norman Nicholson has less force than Mr Gustafson, but he is much more readable and accomplished. He is an interesting mixture: Auden and Wordsworth, regionalism and religion, romanticism and objectivity. His shifts from one mood to another are often extremely moving. He*

> *knows both the past and the present of his county by the Irish Sea, and even his poorer poems are partly salvaged by his eye and memory. In his comprehension of history, legend, and religion, he is superior to Edward Thomas, a better writer within his limitations. His defects are glibness, sentimentality and echoes of other writers. When he is most lyrical he is most monotonous. His feeling for his region is often, as Mr John Crowe Ransom is fond of saying of a great many things, weak-kneed. His blank verse tends to be better than his rhymes; his couplets and terza rima better than his stanzas. Mr Nicholson's quiet sustained abilities can be shown only by long quotations. One poem called "Babylon" is wonderfully fresh and unified and stands out as one of the few satisfactory poems in this whole group...*[345]

What a wonderful opportunity, Lowell seems to have provided here, for a UK publisher or publicist blurb-writer of the time to have quoted selectively that the famous Lowell's opinion of *Five Rivers* was:

> *"Readable and accomplished...*
> *Wonderfully fresh and unified."*

But, even if these snippets were to be put back into their proper context, this would remain a rather glowing commendation, from a world-respected source, and Nicholson must have been very proud indeed to read it, as surely he must have done, although no hard evidence of this appears to survive. Less unassuming individuals than Nicholson would probably have dined out for years on the strength of this particular review, and ensured that it received maximum publicity, but it has remained buried in transatlantic archives for more than sixty years, and it is probably thanks only to the range and power of modern internet search engines that it has ultimately been disinterred.

The observation that Nicholson's work has tended to be appreciated and admired much more by fellow poets than by critics is borne out by all many warm tributes which poured in for his seventieth birthday Festschrift, *Between Comets*. A former Poet Laureate, Sir Andrew Motion (b. 1950) also recognised, over thirty years ago, significant linkages between the poetry of Thomas Hardy and that of Nicholson - Motion wrote:

> *...(Nicholson) provides a body of work which, for all its incidental resemblances to Wordsworth, is really closer to Hardy: it is undeviatingly colloquial, anecdotal and empirical...He has made a virtue of restraint, and its advantage is a poetry of impressive tact.*[346]

Motion concluded, however, that the inevitable consequential flaw, in his opinion (and that of some other, otherwise admiring, critics) is that:

> *...it means he (Nicholson) has to forgo the resonances, elevations and intensities...produced by a sense of the... sublime.*[347]

More recently, the Hardy connection has been considered by David Cooper, who in the course of his PhD research brought this, in the wider context of the poetry of place, to the attention of a Hardy specialist and biographer, Professor Ralph Pite, whose paper titled *Hardy in the Rural*[348] has cited Nicholson as an example, like Hardy himself, of being influenced both by intertextuality and modernist influences and both:

> *...tending to rebuke assumptions often brought to provincial poetry...(to) overturn hierarchies within which both provincial and centre have their allotted place, their assigned style, and their stereotypical mind-set.*[349]

Pite points out that it was Nicholson who chose not to include in his (1982) *Selected Poems* the epic *Bow in the Cloud* or *The Evacuees*, (though he does not mention the omission of Nicholson's topographical but nonetheless fine poem *Five Rivers* in this regard, either). Pite mentions too the omission of *The Blackberry* poem. Not unlike Andrew Motion before him, Pite identifies:-

> *...a concern on Nicholson's part to sustain an image of himself as a provincial poet, within quite a narrow definition of provinciality.*[350]

All this is perhaps illustrative of multiple factors: for example, of Nicholson's tendency to seek to tailor his work to the particular form he considered appropriate to the intended audience, along of course with Nicholson's realisation in later life that too much of his early work had been too overtly and dogmatically religious. Furthermore, Craig Raine (b. 1944) was, by 1981, Poetry Editor at Faber and Faber, and may possibly have exerted his own editorial influence in Nicholson's overtly religious poetry being omitted from the 1982 Faber edition of Nicholson's *Selected Poems*

In 1980, just seven years before his own death, Nicholson wrote an obituary for the Kendal poet Margaret Cropper.[351] The influences of this remarkable lady upon Nicholson's own literary and spiritual life have been mentioned previously in this book, but Nicholson's own (1980) placement of his neighbour's *oeuvre* in the whole context of 20th Century English poetry is perhaps and indirectly deeply revealing of his own self-perceived standing in this regard:

> *...She was of almost the same generation as T. S. Eliot and Ezra Pound, and for much of her life she must have felt that she was writing against the prevailing fashion. In fact it can now be seen that her work belongs to a tradition in English poetry which has endured in spite of all the experiments and. changes - the tradition ofThomas Hardy, Wilfred Owen, Edward Thomas and Andrew Young...*

Nicholson here seems to be identifying himself with the self-same tradition, or counterculture. To his list of exponents of Margaret Cropper's poetic tradition, as well as himself, Nicholson might have added many other names such as: Charles Causley, Jack Clemo and R.S. Thomas. Indeed, it has already been mentioned in the Introduction to this book how very many similarities exist between Nicholson as a poet and Causley.

Particularly notable in this regard is the Causley-inspired commentary of eminent American poet and critic, Dana Gioia. In a (1997) essay / study entitled *The Most Unfashionable Poet Alive* Gioia writes of Causley:

> *...he has mastered an impressive variety of forms and styles. The true unity of his oeuvre depends less on a specific allegiance to any particular form than on his fundamental commitment to certain old-fashioned virtues of English poetry - simplicity, clarity, grace, and compassion. His work also demonstrates a conviction that the traditional forms of popular poetry remain living modes of expression, despite the Modernist revolution...*
>
> *To call Causley's aesthetic conservative, however, fails to describe its radical independence from literary trends. He deserves some designation both more specific and singular to differentiate him from fellow travellers of the counterrevolutionary fifties like Larkin and Amis. They made common cause of agnosticism in face of international Modernism's Great Awakening. They share an intoxication with traditional meters (though all three write superbly in free verse when occasion demands). They recognize the efficiency of a clear narrative line, even in their lyrical utterances. Contrarians all, they came to maturity in the Sturm und*

> *Drang of Dylan Thomas and The New Apocalypse - a feverish milieu that confirmed their native anti-romanticism.*
>
> *Not for working-class Causley, however, was the ironic detachment, emotional reserve, and guarded knowingness of his Oxonian counterparts. Causley possesses an essential innocence that Amis never reveals and Larkin hid under layers of ironic self-deprecation. Although their poetic tastes often coincide–and the three conspicuously share Hardy and Auden as decisive masters–their personalities differ dramatically...*[352]

The common links with Nicholson and other poets such as Margaret Cropper are so very self-evident here as hardly to require further elucidation.

Canon Andrew Young, as mentioned above, was held in high esteem as a poet by Nicholson. Nicholson, in the 1950s, published a detailed critical appraisal of Young as a poet, in part via the Cumbrian Literary Group (C.L.G.) As their title suggests, the C.L.G. was a county-wide association of authors and aspiring authors, with a membership of between 100 and 150, whose members' bulletins were laboriously typed onto duplicator stencils and painfully run-off on a mimeograph machine, Compared with the digitally-originated and desktop-published multicoloured creations of today, the 1950s C.L.G. bulletins thus very much represent the triumph of sheer content over mere format.

The Cumbrian Literary Group had been founded in 1946 by J. Roderick Webb of Flimby, West Cumbria, whose father was the Church of England vicar of that Parish. An appreciative local journal article on Nicholson by Webb survives in Whitehaven County Records Office[353], as does a letter (in a private collection)[354] from Nicholson to his friend S.L. Bethell, in which he mentions that he had spent a weekend at Flimby with 'Rodry Webb' during which they had toured Maryport, Holm Coultram; Silloth and Allonby, all of which places, Nicholson remarks in the letter, were new to him.

Nicholson himself was an active C.L.G. member and supporter; in 1957, the Group's President was George Bott (1920-2002), the Keswick-based schoolteacher and author, whilst the Vice-President was another widely published author and journalist, Dudley Hoys of the Woolpack Inn in Eskdale (which, probably far from coincidentally, was where Nicholson and his new wife Yvonne spent their honeymoon, in 1956). The other Vice-President was Graham Sutton (1892-1959), the then very well known and popular Cumbrian novelist and poet. George Bott remained the Group's President for nearly fifty years; until his death, Bott was a longstanding friend and staunch champion of Nicholson's work.

There appeared in a 1957 Cumbrian Literary Group Bulletin an extensive critical review by Nicholson of the poetry of Andrew Young (1885-1971).[355]

(Like Nicholson, Young's passion, apart from poetry, was wild flowers, and during the 1940s Young had published several prose books, including two devoted to British wild plants.)

Nicholson, in his unique style, begins his discussion with a discourse on something he sees as self-evident – that Young is a 'modern' poet, his work belonging to the same world and idiom as Eliot and Auden:

> *...like Edward Thomas and Robert Frost he has moved away from the empty, pretty jingles of the Georgian poets towards the language of real speech...He takes to nature something of the same gentle wit that George Herbert took to religion.*

Exactly the same characteristics and antecedents of course apply to Norman Nicholson's own poetry, which perhaps explains Nicholson's deep interest in Young's poetry and his obvious affinity with it.

One extract, from a Young poem, *Hard Frost*, may illustrate this:

> *In the hard-rutted lane*
> *At every footstep breaks a brittle pane,*
> *And tinkling trees ice-bound,*
> *Changed into weeping willows, sweep the ground*
> ...
> *But vainly the fierce frost*
> *Interns poor fish, ranks trees in an armed host,*
> *Hangs daggers from house-eaves*
> *And on the windows ferny ambush weaves;*
> *In the long war grown warmer*
> *The sun will strike him dead and strip his armour.*

Nicholson's study quotes a number of other examples, making the point that most of Young's poems are built around a single idea, or 'conceit'. Nicholson observes:

> *...the conceit is not merely a display of virtuosity, not merely a decoration; it is the very impulse from which the poem springs as naturally as a daffodil from a bulb. It is developed and brought to its flowering in the fewest possible words and once this has been done, the poem is over – if there are any deeper implications, as often there are, the reader is left to discover them for himself...*

Nicholson might of course have been speaking of his own poetry too, and indeed of 'modern' poetry in general.

Nicholson turns to Young's detachment from his verse, calling this his 'objectivity':

> *...In so far as he enters his own poem it is merely as the instrument which records. Even when the incident is purely personal, one which happens in the poet's mind and not in the world at all, it is still told with the same objectivity...*

Again, one can make a direct linkage to Nicholson's own views. In the poem *From a Boat at Coniston* Nicholson pondered a very similar theme:

> *...I wait for the wind to drop, against hope*
> *Hoping, and against the weather, yet to see*

The water empty, the water full of itself,
Free of the sky and the cloud and free of me.

Nicholson stresses too in his commentary on Young, that he and fellow - 'moderns' cannot now escape in full from urban civilization and all its influences: the countryside around us will never again be as it was for the boy Wordsworth or for the young John Clare: Man is now an interloper within the world of Nature, but, paradoxically, 'moderns' like Young (and Nicholson?) use this same separation as a means of scrutinising it all very closely indeed, sometimes uncomfortably so.

Direct linkages are perhaps evident too, as regards Nicholson's own affinity with the religious underpinnings of Young's poetry:

> *...Behind his love of the created world there is of course a Christian belief in the Creator, but this is never thrust in the reader's face. Perhaps he feels that if people are to see sermons in stones they must be persuaded first of all to look at the stones...*

This remark in particular chimes with the fact noted on multiple occasions within this book[356] that in later life Nicholson came to regret the extent to which his own youthful religious ardour had been reflected in his poetry and other works, such as the plays. Perhaps, even as early as 1957, this element of regret was taking hold in Nicholson's mind, inspired by Young's example.

One final similarity between Nicholson and Young is that the poetry of both of them has been generally deeply unfashionable and virtually ignored, save by more perceptive critics, these often being poets themselves. One of the few exceptions to this 'Poet's Poet' syndrome, though, was Craig Raine (b. 1944, and no relation to the eponymous Kathleen) who became poetry editor at Faber and Faber in 1981, where he remained until 1991. Little documentary evidence exists as regards Raine's critical opinion of Nicholson as a poet, save for one very telling letter, written by Raine to Nicholson's literary agents about a suggestion that Nicholson's *oeuvre* be published by Faber and Faber, wholly or partially, as a 'Collected' edition.

In 1984, Raine himself had contributed a poem to Nicholson's *Between Comets Festschrift*, and a little earlier must have edited Nicholson's *Selected Poems 1940 - 1982*. (Nicholson's last poetry collection, *Sea to the West*, was probably already completely through the editing stage prior to Raine joining Faber.)

Raine's letter is quite critical of Nicholson as a poet. It contains a mixture of very limited and polite admiration and of even fainter praise for Nicholson's literary achievements, which he is adamant would be diminished, rather than enhanced, by any future volume of collected poems. He criticises Nicholson for having taken too long to disentangle his own poetic voice from those of Eliot and Auden, whilst Raine considered Nicholson's verse drama to be outdated as well as merely derivative of that of Eliot.

Raine said too that he feared that airing more of Nicholson's earlier poetry would simply result in Nicholson becoming side-lined as just another minor poet. Larkin's earlier poetry, Raine asserts, can withstand informed critical scrutiny, but Raine considers that Nicholson's simply cannot. Raine mentions in a postscript that he has talked the matter over with Charles Monteith[357] (1921-1995) who has in fact persuaded Raine to sanction a Collected Poems only (i.e. omitting the plays) and then only provided that the estimated costs and projected sales might justify going ahead with the project.

Raine reports that all subsequent indications were that the project would almost certainly not be commercially viable, so it had indeed been dropped.

Christopher Reid (b. 1949) succeeded Raine at Fabers in 1991 and the Nicholson Lobby must have breathed heavy sighs of relief and resumed their entreaties, culminating in the (1994) publication of Nicholson's *Collected Poems,* edited by Nicholson's friend and fellow local poet, Neil Curry.

Since *Collected Poems,* as well as the collective endeavours of The Norman Nicholson Society and of its founder Chairman, Dr. David Cooper, there have been glimmerings of further scholarly interest in Nicholson. For example, interest from Andrew Gibson who is Research Professor of Modern Literature and Theory in the English Department, at Royal Holloway, University of London. Gibson recently delivered a talk at Trinity College, Dublin on Nicholson, entitled: *'At the Dying Atlantic's Edge':*

Norman Nicholson and the Cumbrian Coast.[358]

Gibson comments that '*something rather special springs*' from a poet of Nicholson's prowess choosing to inhabit and to write about such a marginal and (in most part) strangely bleak area. This area Gibson terms 'The Atlantic Edge' - the West and South-West Cumbrian coastal plain which lies 'betwixt the mountains and the sea' and which, in the starkest possible contrast with the main English Lake District, is generally an unlovely and unloved and unvisited post-Industrial wasteland.

Gibson observes that:

> *The space of the Atlantic edge fairly comprehensively determines the character of Nicholson's vision and the substance of what he has to say...*

He continues:

> *In effect, for Nicholson, there is no coastal culture. In this respect, he separates himself, not only from the Lake poets, but from the whole tradition of English 'provincial' poetry (Crabbe, Clare, Hardy, early Lawrence) to which his work has more often been linked. Historically, then, too, this is a land of detritus, the incoherent offscourings of history.*

Gibson has experienced at length and personally the Millom town environment and that of other West Cumbrian post-industrial settlements. He fully realises that but for the demands of the First Industrial Revolution, these places simply would not exist, and that the very reason for their existence has now disappeared along with their former industries. They hardly, even in their heyday, possessed any tradition of their own, and have even less now that they are in decline. Thus there stands a Millom with no ironworks and no culture of its own, other than that which was imported by its immigrant industrial workers from elsewhere. Similarly, stand places further north, such as Cleator Moor; Moor Row, Pica and very many others. This perhaps explains too, why, to a Millomite or a Barrovian for example, the world beyond the boundaries of their home town, even though still within Cumbria, might just as well be another, faraway, mysterious foreign country[359]: there is little sense of wider regional or indigenous cultural tradition here. Even 'the Atlantic Edge' is itself just a name or an unknown construct.

Nicholson's poetry is described as messianic by Gibson:

> *...in some of the poems, God sends the Atlantic spilling over its edge into the wasteland, not only or even chiefly destructively or in wrath, but as a messianic image of radical justice. Nicholson's conception of the Atlantic edge is as an absolute boundary which forces the mind to think the impossible, vertical transaction, of which the idea of justice is a principal manifestation...*

The Bow in the Cloud is perhaps the biggest manifestation of this aspect of Nicholson's poetry, but, in one of novels, the character Benjy in *The Fire of the Lord* is plainly messianic too, the consuming cataclysmic element in his case being fire and not water, whilst the other novel *The Green Shore* is in essence a survey of Nicholson's native Edgeland: a commentary upon the character Anthony's (and, indirectly, Mankind's) doomed, tormented quest for Heaven on Earth, or for that 'garden by the sea.'

Gibson concludes and summates his perceptive analysis thus:

> *...Nicholson rethinks his territory in and through his vision of devastation, but also as a landscape that requires the impossible redemption. This, together with the boy's love of poetry and his seduction by the beauty of a religious language, establishes the core of his poetry as messianic. Nicholson's poetic thought as a whole and the rest of the poetry are substantially organized around this core.*

Nicholson's poetic technique, specifically his artifice with rhyme, has recently been analysed in an academic paper delivered to a conference at Durham University by Dr Stacey McDowell of Bristol University.[360] McDowell discusses the considerable subtleties and intricacies deployed by Nicholson in linking rhyme both with meaning and movement of focus within his poems, with particular consideration of *The Blackberry* and *Wall*. This is interesting too, as regards Nicholson's early poetical technique: the former is a very early Nicholson poem and the latter a much later one, yet the considerable rhyming skill was present from the start, and continued apace, rather than gradually developing via greater experience.

Other recent interest in Nicholson has included the deployment of sophisticated visualisation computer software to analyse and, in new and rather arresting ways, graphically to illustrate the scope and coverage of Nicholson's very extensive network of literary friends and contacts.[361] This in itself provides ample further evidence for the close networking which existed in such circles, but of course a basic limitation is that it can only analyse surviving Nicholson correspondence. For example, Nicholson's extensive correspondence with Bessie Satterthwaite (Schiff); Sylvia Lubelsky; George Every and Enrica is not fully or hardly included, simply because Nicholson deliberately destroyed it before his death.

Nearly thirty years ago, just two years before Nicholson's death, Peter Swaab published an adroitly-balanced critical overview of Nicholson's poetic *oeuvre* in *The Cambridge Review.*[362] In this, he acknowledges the early virtuosity of *Five Rivers,* commenting that '*Five Rivers*', despite its apparent simplicity at first reading, is:

> *...organised beyond straightforwardness.*
> *And, echoing Kathleen Raine, he observes that:*
> *...the presence of Eliot is often felt, sometimes*
> *in lines which echo his later lugubriousness...*

Swaab recognizes Nicholson's originality and technical skill with rhythm and metre, which he considers is very much lacking in for example Craig Raine's own poetry!

In a fine and balanced conclusion, Swaab says:

> *Although I have been drawn to compare Nicholson's art with Eliot's and Wordsworth's, his poems assign themselves a more modest place. His confidence in the channels of communication between poet and reader sets him apart from the mainstream of twentieth century poetry…*

On that resounding note, perhaps it is appropriate to conclude this study.

Epilogue

It is now well over 25 years since Nicholson's death: sufficient 'critical distance' adequately to evaluate his worth and standing as a poet, but, conversely, something of an impediment to piecing together the story of his quiet yet colourful life.

If I have succeeded even in small part in either of these endeavours, I shall be more than pleased, and I am moved to end with repeated note of very sincere and most grateful thanks to all those who have helped me in any way upon this truly fascinating and fulfilling journey of discovery.

Index

C

D

E

F

G

H

I

J

K

N

O

P

Q

R

S

Endnotes

1. Merged with Westmorland and parts of other adjacent counties in 1974 into the new county of Cumbria.
2. With BBC Radio Cumbria (1970s).
3. NICHOLSON, N. (1975) *Wednesday, Early Closing*, Faber & Faber, London. (Hereinafter referenced as *'WEC'*).
4. Hereinafter referenced as 'Gardner's thesis.'
5. GARDNER, P.G., (1973) *Norman Nicholson* (Twayne's English Authors, 153), Twayne, New York – hereinafter referenced as 'Gardner's book'.
6. Gardner's book, end note 32, page 163.
7. GIOIA, D, *The Most Unfashionable Poet Alive: Charles Causley* [online]. Available from: http://www.danagioia.net/essays/ecausley.htm. [Accessed: 1 September, 2013].
8. JONES, K. (2013) *Norman Nicholson: The Whispering Poet*, The Book Mill, Cumbria (hereinafter referenced as 'Jones' biography'.
9. The magnificent remains of the furnace at Duddon Bridge (near Millom) exemplify this.
10. Not unlike the Duddon Furnace.
11. The British Steel Corporation had pilot plants too, at Shelton, Stoke on Trent, and at Irlam, Manchester, but the process was never taken further, either in the UK, or elsewhere in the world.

12. Iron and Steel Bill, House of Lords Deb. 13 February 1967 vol. 280 cc41-146
13. Refers to the late Dr D.R.G, 'Robson' Davies, whose kind help and encouragement with this section is gratefully acknowledged.
14. LANCASTER, J.Y. AND WATTLEWORTH, D.R., (1977) *The Iron and Steel Industry of West Cumbria: An Historical Survey,* Workington, .British Steel Corporation. (Chapter 10).
15. E.g., Nicholson's poem *'Windscale'* (as the Sellafield nuclear plant was once called).
16. And repeated in Jones' biography.
17. The collective noun being a rake of wagons.
18. Poignantly, a small chunk of Millom spray steel survives in the care of the town's Museum.
19. Interspersed with 'slagging' – discharging the slag which floated upon the surface of the molten iron, within the furnace hearth.
20. Casting in sand pig beds was supplanted both at Millom and throughout the industry by pig casting machinery, a continuous moulding and water-spray solidification process.
21. Some other skilled workers, such as Foundry Patternmakers, moved upon closure further up the Cumbrian coast to Workington, into employment with Distington Engineering Company, which was then the biggest iron foundry in Europe. The company provided housing, too, for these key workers.
22. From unscientific observation, but based upon strong impression.
23. Known in the industry as the 'Bear' or 'Salamander'
24. Issue 2349, April 04, 1974, pp 437-431 – most of the letters were written to John Edward Fisher.
25. Called (appropriately) at that time *Sealand Hovercraft*.
26. The 'Look, Stranger' title of course alluding to W.H. Auden's poem.
27. SECKER, S. (1975) Review of *WEC* in *The Times Literary Supplement* (London, England). Friday, November 21.

28. Rylands catalogue ref. MSN/1/58.

29. The poet Charles Causley reviewed *WEC* for *The Guardian,* and, doubtless thinking of Laurie Lee, rather acutely and tartly observed that Nicholson *avoids carefully a 'poetic' prose made ghastly by the corpses of half-buried poems.*

30. A choice of pseudonym perhaps deliberate and potentially very revealing of Nicholson's feelings for Sylvia. It may have been deliberately chosen by Nicholson as pertaining to Charles Williams' adoption of the name as symbolic of ideal love; of love for another human being as a path towards at least some glimpses of God's divine love. This derived from Williams' study of Dante's Beatrice (1943), with which Nicholson was very familiar. See too: Charles Williams, ed., *The New Book of English Verse* (London: Gollancz, 1935), pp 12–15, and Williams, C. *The Figure of Beatrice: A Study in Dante* (London: Faber and Faber, 1943), pp 49–51.

31. The University of Manchester John Rylands Library holds the actual letters; I am indebted to the late Sylvia Lubelsky's daughter, Mrs Jacqui Monty, for her kind help.

32. Maurice Elvey had himself been a Linford Sanatorium patient, alongside Sylvia.

33. University of Exeter, *The Cornish in Latin America* [online]. Available from: http://projects.exeter.ac.uk/cornishlatin/pachucarealdelmonte.htm. [Accessed 28 September, 2013].

34. White Star Line, *RMS Olympic Passenger List, dep. Southampton, March 13, 1912 (1278 passengers)* [online]. Available from: http://www.titanic1.org/articles/pdfs/crossing9-march13-20-1912-v2.pdf [Accessed 28 September, 2013].

35. THWAITE, A., (2004) Nicholson, Norman Cornthwaite (1914–1987), entry in *Oxford Dictionary of National Biography*, Oxford University Press, Oxford.

36. In *WEC,* Nicholson mentions that surgical collapsing of TB-infected lungs was practised at Linford, but had been ruled-out by the doctors in his particular case.

37. The fees, in 2013 monetary values, would have amounted to between about £500 a week based solely on retail price inflation and substantially more than £2000 a week, fully taking into account increased national prosperity.

38. As in the biological process termed 'imprinting' in animals.

39. Which largely inspired his (1943) published book, *Man and Literature*, and, indirectly, too, his first published poetry collection, *Five Rivers.*

40. Quoted in Gardner's thesis.

41. In a private collection

42. *North-Western Evening Mail*, 24 November, 1977

43. E.g., to Philip Gardner, in particular.

44. Unpublished Paper: STRUDWICK, V. *Religious Communities and the Big Society:* A presentation to the International Theology Summer Programme at Christ Church, Oxford, 2011.

45. For example his novel *The Green Shore* and his *Millom Revisited* article in *The Listener.*

46. The serious and debilitating effects of this attack of influenza were, coincidentally, mentioned in a (unpublished) letter from Nicholson to his (and Every's friend, S.L. Bethell.

47. NICHOLSON, N. (Editor), (1942), *An Anthology of Religious Verse*, Harmondsworth, England, Penguin Book (hereinafter 'his anthology of religious verse').

48. SPURR, B., (2010) (*Anglo-Catholic in Religion: T.S. Eliot and Christianity, London,* Lutterworth Press.

49. Expressed in a private email to this author.

50. Letter from Every to Nicholson, Manchester University Rylands Library, Papers of Norman Cornthwaite Nicholson, Catalogue ref NBK/81.

51. Nicholson, around the same period, on at least one occasion stayed as Kathleen Raine's house guest, in her Chelsea home. St. Anne's may possibly have been the purpose of Nicholson's London visit on this occasion, but at present no concrete evidence exists.

52. Jones' biography alleges that Nicholson's friendship with them waned during this period, for which there is no evidence (and indeed, much indication of the converse).

53. During wartime, probably entailing a train journey from Millom to Workington, then changing onto the line linking Workington and Penrith, via Cockermouth and Keswick.

54. See Gardner Thesis, p.303 (footnote).

55. Married name: Henrietta Dombey, who was Professor of Literacy in Primary Education, at Brighton University.

56. Now Sir Adam Roberts, KCMG, former Professor of International Relations, Oxford University.

57. Information most kindly provided to the author by Mrs Anna Hopewell.

58. Latterly, he was Professor, History of Africa, at the University of London.

59. ROBERTS, A. D. (Editor) (2000) *Janet Adam Smith Remembered,* London, privately-published, p. 21 (contribution by Dombey, Daniel (Janet's grandson)).

60. I am indebted to Lord Clement-Jones for his kind provision of this part of his family history data, (along with his pithy observations regarding intermarriage of cousins in Victorian times).

61. - Gardner Thesis, pp 59 & 60.

62. 9 November, 1956, p. 9

63. GARDNER, P (1973*) Norman Nicholson (Twayne's English Authors Series)* New York, Twayne Publishers Inc.

64. from her English mother

65. See Janet Martin / Norman Nicholson papers, Manchester University Rylands Library.

66. Biographical information from a Walthamstow Hall School Old Girls Association obituary to Enrica (extract undated but probably c. 1991)

67. Homerton College records

68. Eltham College being its counterpart for boys.

69. Claremont School archives

70. Ibid.
71. During which Enrica regardless of her own safety, supervised and calmed the boarders.
72. LINDOP, G. 1995 'In Conversation with Anne Ridler' *PN Review* 101,Volume 21 Number 3
73. Jones' biography repeats this supposition.
74. SCM Archives, held by Cadbury Special Collections, University of Birmingham Library.
75. E.g., letters from Enrica to Every, quoted in Gardner thesis
76. Surviving picture postcards, (dated 1944) K. Raine to Nicholson, Manchester University Rylands Library, catalogue ref NCN/13.
77. Ibid.
78. Gardner thesis
79. Kindly supplied by one of the wartime evacuee pupils
80. The contrast between Shining Cranesbill and one of Nicholson's favourite local wild flowers, the Bloody Cranesbill is doubtless coincidental but nonetheless rather eerie.
81. Private information
82. Somewhat archaic colloquialism for a jobbing newspaper reporter, charged with covering all manner of mundane events.
83. Detailed citation would be highly inappropriate here but this information has been triangulated from multiple sources.
84. Jones' biography states that the reason for the break-up was Nicholson's unwillingness to move away from Millom, but cites no evidence for this suggestion.
85. T.S. Eliot's own marriage two years earlier, to Valerie Fletcher, his secretary at Faber and Faber, was of course a similar event.
86. Only a (formerly-unidentified) portrait photo of Enrica as a young woman remains.
87. MARSH, R. & TAMBIMUTTU (Eds.) (1948) *T.S. Eliot: A Symposium* London P.L. Editions.

88. SMART, D., *John Fisher at Mexborough Grammar School:* A Memoir. Available from: http://joseflocke.co.uk/heritage/MGS02.htm. [Accessed 2 October, 2013].

89. REID, C. (Ed.), (2008), *Letters of Ted Hughes*, New York: Farrar, Straus and Giroux.

90. Ibid.

91. An incident also recalled by Nicholson himself, in a 1970s BBC Radio Cumbria interview.

92. Dramatized by Lee Hall in his eponymous 2011 play.

93. No firm evidence for this conjecture exists, however.

94. Kathleen Raine's own nearby location, at Martindale Old Vicarage, was equally magnificent (albeit even more rugged and remote.)

95. UNIVERSITY OF THE THIRD AGE, PENRITH (1998), *Michael Roberts, Janet Adam Smith, and Kathleen Raine: Three Writers in Penrith and Martindale during World War II,* privately-published booklet. (Hereinafter 'U3A Study' accessed in Penrith Museum, 2013))

96. T.S. Eliot is described in Jones' biography as having met up with Nicholson himself at Cockley Moor in 1942, but no evidence for this exists, other than of this single brief visit accompanied by the Roberts's.

97. Ibid above.

98. CORBETT, V. (1996), *A Rhythm A Rite and a Ceremony: Helen Sutherland at Cockley Moor 1939-1965*, Penrith: Midnight Oil

99. Ibid above

100. Rylands Library ref. GB 133 NCN/13.

101. See BLAMIRES. D., (1971), *David Jones: Artist & Writer*, Ilkley, The Scholar Press.

102. Page 61.

103. Rylands ref NCN1/1/82; letter from HS dated 14 January, 1965.

104. CROSS, D.A. (2007), *Cumbrian Brothers: Letters from Percy Kelly to Norman Nicholson* Carlisle, Fell Foot Press.

105. Ibid.

106. Freer's papers are retained in Manchester University John Rylands Library, ref GB 133 AFR but unfortunately are not yet catalogued.

107. CORBETT, V. (1996), *A Rhythm A Rite and a Ceremony: Helen Sutherland at Cockley Moor 1939-1965*, Penrith, Midnight Oil.

108. As in *Tradition and the Individual Talent.*

109. In a 1970s BBC local radio interview.

110. Obituary, Peter Forbes, *The Observer*, 28 October, 2001

111. GORDON, R. (2007) 'Ridler, Anne Barbara (1912–2001)', *Oxford Dictionary of National Biography*, Oxford: Oxford University Press.

112. See too Chapter Nine.

113. BETHELL S.L. (1944) Shakespeare *& Dramatic Tradition,* London, Staples Press.

114. ELIOT, T.S. (1921) *The Sacred Wood,* New York, Alfred A. Knopf.

115. BETHELL S.L. (1944) *Shakespeare & Popular Dramatic Tradition*, London, Staples Press.

116. BETHELL S.L. (1943) *The Literary Outlook,* London, Sheldon Press.

117. Ibid.

118. Ibid.

119. Trained as a skilled torpedo and underwater weapons mechanic, and deployed at all land-based naval establishments which handled torpedo armaments.

120. Browne was T.S. Eliot's verse play Producer, see too chapter 9.

121. Mitchell, W.R., feature article in *Cumbria* magazine, May, 1986 p.92-95.

122. This, and much related information, from an article by Yvonne's sister, Joyce, Rosemary (Mrs) in NN Soc. Journal *Comet* (2009) Volume 4 No. 1

123. See Nicholson's poem *Epithalamium for a Niece.*

124. Appropriately for Nicholson, the name (pronounced 'Ree-ah' is said to derive from Norse for 'the bend in the river.
125. Letter from Nicholson to Daniel Hay, dated 24 February 1966: County Archives, Whitehaven, Cumbria.
126. Nicholson warmly and gratefully dedicated his (1969) book *Greater Lakeland* to the Eckersleys.
127. Letter to David and Pippa Wright from Nicholson, Manchester University Rylands Library, ref. GB 133 DPW/1/6, dated 1 October, 1967.
128. Ibid.
129. Prearranged by Yvonne before she died.
130. Rylands Library, letter from Nicholson to Matt Simpson dated 5 November, 1982, catalogue ref. MSN/1/52.
131. HAY, D. (1967) Norman Nicholson *Library Review* 21 (1) p. 5 - 9
132. Ibid, p. 5 (Of course, these comments preceded Nicholson's later poetry collections, *A Local Habitation* and *Sea to the West*, but these probably would not have changed Hay's strong opinion.
133. Now held by Cumbria County Council Archives Office, Whitehaven, Cumbria.
134. Beginning in 1946, when Hay wrote to Nicholson offering his help with topics West Cumbrian having seen in a press article that Nicholson was to researching his *Cumberland and Westmorland* topographical book.
135. *Whitehaven News*, 19 June, 1954
136. Presumably the poem 'Five Rivers'.
137. For example, Millom's own town council typically were not inclined to honour Nicholson other than with rather faint and grudging praise (see eg Chapter 7).
138. To Daniel Hay, dated 5 December, 1967, in Whitehaven, Cumbria County Archives Office.
139. (various authors) (1964) *Writers on Themselves*, London, BBC Publications (pages 1 to 7)
140. Hardy's novel of course comes to mind, here.

141. See Nicholson's contribution to MORGAN, Dewi (Ed.) (1966) *They Became Christians,* Mowbray, London
142. Recounted in Gardner thesis, p. 63 et seq.
143. Vol. 51, No. 6, March, 1938
144. Vol.53, No. 4
145. Who later became intensely interested in World War II poetry.
146. See: TOLLEY, A.T. (1985) *The Poetry of the Forties* Manchester, Manchester University Press. (Although Tolley makes no mention of *Bolero* as the forerunner of *Kingdom Come.)*
147. Coincidentally, a sociological research technique founded by Charles Madge, who was an early husband of Kathleen Raine.
148. *Daily Telegraph* obituary.
149. Gardner thesis, p. 80
150. Ibid
151. London, July 10, 1942, p. 385
152. Gardner thesis, p. 68 et seq.
153. Where Bessie Satterthwaite was the Branch Secretary.
154. Subsequently reprinted in the journal *Theology* No. 40, June, 1940.
155. QV
156. E.g. the poem, *'Cleator Moor'.*
157. Chapter 7 continues this account.
158. It survived Beeching etc., and remains a passenger rail link in 2013: one of the most scenic rail journeys to be experienced anywhere in England.
159. Gardner thesis, page 84.
160. Nicholson, by then an established freelance journalist, used the experience for an article in the magazine *Time and Tide* (Vol. 35, 24 July, 1954 pp. 987-988)
161. Chapter 13
162. Nicholson himself spoke of this during a 1970s BBC Local Radio interview.

163. MERCER, D. (1984) 'Local Profile: Norman Nicholson' *West Cumberland Advertiser*, 8 June.

164. NICHOLSON, N. (1985) ('In Conversation with David Wright' *PN Review* 46, Vol 12, No.2, November / December.

165. For further discussion please see Chapter 13.

166. The sculptress Josefina de Vasconcellos (also known then as Mrs Delmar Banner), Nicholson's close friend, had herself produced a (pre-side-whiskers) 'younger' head, many years previously.

167. Another casting of the same is held by Manchester University John Rylands Library.

168. Millom News, 6 July, 1984.

169. The author is very grateful to the former custodian of the late George Every's papers - Mr Bernard Hamilton - for most generously donating this book.

170. A Nicholson poem, recalling both himself as a shy child, and his own very forthright grandmother.

171. An allusion, of course, to Linford T.B. Sanatorium

172. CF Nicholson's own eponymous poem.

173. Ulverston-based poet and writer, who edited Nicholson's *Collected Poems* for Faber and Faber

174. As early as the end of 1944, Nicholson was expecting the proofs of his second novel from the publishers (letter Nicholson to S.L. Bethell dated 26 December, 1944 (letter in private ownership).

175. Published in *New English Weekly*, 15 September, 1938.

176. Obvious (albeit tenuous) links here to Nicholson's own psychological development and real life circumstances.

177. Nicholson remained an admirer and recreational reader of this author throughout his entire life (source: BBC local radio interview).

178. Gardner thesis, p. 131

179. An iron foundry occupation, in effect a high-precision woodworker, who constructs the mould patterns from which

castings are formed by foundry moulding: a typical Barrow in Furness occupation, during the early 20th Century, and quite a highly-skilled and well-paid one.

180. NICHOLSON, N. (1964) *'Enjoying it all'* London, Waltham Forest Books (page 6).

181. She is not named here, for reasons of confidentiality.

182. QV

183. As well as in many of his later poems.

184. Gardner, p. 31; mentioned too that Nicholson had recently been commissioned to write a verse play for the Pilgrim Players and that Nicholson was minded to write a play about Elijah.

185. Browne, E.M. & H (1981) *Two in One.* Cambridge, U.K.: Cambridge University Press (general source for this Chapter of E. Martin Browne-related biographical information)

186. Ibid. (Chapter 8,p. 153)

187. Recounted by Irvine Hunt, in his obituary article to Nicholson in *Cumberland News*, Friday 5 June, 1987 (page 7).

188. In a 1970s BBC Radio Cumbria Interview.

189. Now known as 'Radius'.

190. Browne himself replaced Bishop Bell as Hon. President of the Society, in 1938.

191. Then the 'Council for the Encouragement of Music and the Arts (CEMA)'

192. In Genesis, 6-9.

193. Cumbrian dialect for streams or brooks.

194. Firstly, in critical articles in *The Times,* 14 September, 1945 and in the *Daily Telegraph* of 15 September, 1945.

195. Issue 2310, May 11, 1946, p. 224.

196. As Act three opens.

197. The first being by The Unnamed Society at Manchester's Whitworth Theatre, in 1947 (see Gardner thesis, p.333).

198. RICKERBY, Valerie (2013), article in Norman Society Journal *Comet,* Volume 7 Issue 3, pp 2 &3.

199. See too Chapter 13.2.

200. STRUDWICK, V. (2003) 'George Every – Obituary' *Church Times*, 19 September, p. 24.

201. CROPPER, M. and NICHOLSON, N. (1978) *Something and Everything* Kendal, Abbot Hall Gallery.

202. REED, H. (1946) 'New Poetic Drama', *The Listener,* April 11.

203. Gardner thesis pp. 586-587.

204. Gardner thesis, p. 367 (footnote).

205. Holborn Hill is the name of the original rural hamlet from which the industrialised town of Millom grew.

206. Thursday, September 28, 1950; pg. 433; Issue 1130.

207. Gardner thesis, p. 386 (footnote).

208. The sinister aridity of e.g. many major battlefields and in particular preserved Nazi Concentration camp sites is a similar phenomenon.

209. But first acted in 1953.

210. Page 397.

211. QV.

212. NICHOLSON, N. (1953) 'The Comic Prophet' *The Listener*, 6 August, p.222.

213. NICHOLSON, N. (1952) 'Millom Delivered' *The Listener*, 24 January, p. 138.

214. Vol. 33, No. 31, 2 August, 1952.

215. The author is indebted to Mrs Margaret Wiedemann Hunt, Hon Archivist of 'Radius' and Editor of *Radius Performing* for sight of this unique document.

216. KEILY, P (1986). *Memoirs.* Leeds: Privately published. P44-45 – hereinafter 'Keily'.

217. One of the mainline London rail termini.

218. Gardner thesis.

219. London, September 06, 1953; pg. 9; Issue 6803.

220. Charles Williams' influences might be seen here.

221. Correspondence from Denison to Nicholson survives in form of a letter held by Rylands Library ref GB 133 NCN1/1/34

222. June 22, 1954.

223. COOKMAN, Anthony Victor (1955) 'The Prophet's Wife' *Times Literary Supplement,* London, England] 12 Aug.

224. Keily, p.76.

225. Keily, p.59.

226. See above, Gardner's thesis lists the various performances of Nicholson's plays, but omits this particular one.

227. *Cumberland News* article (1954), 15 February.

228. See Gardner thesis, p. 398.

229. Echoing, once more, Charles Williams' views on the matter.

230. Of the Church of England.

231. Replaced by a Punch and Judy Show and a brass band concert.

232. Information most kindly supplied by the current Prior, Oswin Gartside.

233. 17 July, 1959.

234. Mirfield is in the West Riding of Yorkshire, equidistant from Huddersfield and Dewsbury.

235. Letter, Pamela Keily to Philip Gardner, cited on p. 439 of his thesis.

236. Nicholson's own words, cited by Gardner in his thesis, p. 439 (footnote 2).

237. Friday, July 08, 1960; pg. 435; Issue 3045.

238. Gardner thesis, too, mentions subsequent performances by Keily's Players, in Manchester and in Sheffield (p.454).

239. Keily, p. 99.

240. Gardner thesis p.454.

241. p.5.

242. NICHOLSON, N. (1948) 'The Poet Needs an Audience' *Orpheus,* John Lehmann. London,Vol.1 pp 147-154.

243. Ibid.

244. 17th Century English dramatist.

245. See too Chapter 3.10 re S.L. Bethell's work on dramatic tradition and his influential critique of naturalism.

246. John Heath-Stubbs contributed a moving tribute to his fellow poet and friend in the same issue (*Aquarius* (1987) Nos. 17/18).

247. 'Interview (Norman) Nicholson with David Wright' (1985) *PN Review* 46,Vol. 12 No.2.

248. Now Radio Four and Radio Three.

249. NICHOLSON, N. (1943). *Man and Literature.* London: S.C.M. Press.

250. EVERY, G. (1940) *Christian Discrimination*, London, The Sheldon Press.

251. BETHELL, S.L. (1943) *The Literary Outlook (The Christian News-Letter Books, No. 17)* London,The Sheldon Press.

252. LEAVIS, Q.D. (1968) A Selection From Scrutiny Cambridge University Press, pp. 153-158.

253. Fausset, Hugh I'Anson Modern Values: Liberal Man and Natural Man. *Times Literary Supplement* 18 Dec. 1943.

254. Or perhaps at least partially as a result of wartime conditions.

255. NICHOLSON, N, (1940) 'Morals and the Modern Novel'. *Theology*. 40, pp412-420.

256. With most grateful thanks to the late Mr Bethell's family.

257. Further evidenced by correspondence between Charles Williams and George Every (see Chapter 3.02).

258. In: *The Listener*, (London, England), Thursday, November 25, 1943; pg. 618; Issue 776.

259. SCOTT, D.'Cowper's Tame Hare'(2007) Norman Nicholson Society Journal, *Comet Volume 2, Issue 2*.

260. NICHOLSON, N. (1951) *William Cowper* London John Lehmann.

261. NICHOLSON, N. (Ed.) (1975) *A Choice of Cowper's Verse* London, Faber & Faber.

262. NICHOLSON, N. Ed.) (1951) *Selected Poems of William Cowper* London, Grey Walls Press.

263. A prominent literary figure of the time, who also published the 1940s literary journal *Poetry Quarterly* and a number of Nicholson poems therein.

264. Available from: http://findingaids.library.emory.edu/documents/gardiner641/ [accessed 2 June, 2014].

265. Although stresses that the link cannot be evidenced.

266. Pages 61 and 62 (further indication, too, that the reason given in Jones' biography is supposition only).

267. Page 16

268. Page 19

269. CURRY, N. (2011) *William and Theodora: An Early Love Affair - [An edited version of a talk given by the author at the Cowper Day held in Olney on 10 September 2011]*. Available from: http://www.cowperandnewtonmuseum.org.uk/wp-content/uploads/2013/01/William-and-Theadora.pdf [accessed 2 November 2013]...

270. BRUNSTRÖM, C. (2006) 'Leaving the Herd-How Queer was Cowper?' *British Journal for Eighteenth-Century Studies*, 29 pp 157-167.

271. Cf., too, perhaps, Kathleen Raine's attachment to Gavin Maxwell and Josefina de Vasconcellos' to Delmar Banner (both of them homosexuals).

272. In the academic, 'sexual diversity studies' sense of this term.

273. NICHOLSON, N. (1949) *Wordsworth – An Introduction and a Selection,* London, Phoenix House

274. MARSH, R. & TAMBIMUTTU (Eds.) (1948) *T.S. Eliot: A Symposium*, London, P.L. Editions.

275. NICHOLSON, N (1950) The two William Wordsworths, *Picture Post* Saturday, April 22, 1950; pg. 32; Issue 4.

276. Ibid.

277. In 'The friend'

278. NICHOLSON, N. (1949) *Wordsworth – An Introduction and a Selection*, London, Phoenix House

279. Page 38

280. Page 192

281. NICHOLSON, N (1950) H.G. Wells, London, Arthur Barker Ltd.

282. Available from: http://www.britannica.com/EBchecked/topic/639453/HG-Wells [last accessed: 3 June, 2014]

283. BRONTE, Charlotte (1947) *Wuthering Heights* (Camden Classics Edition) London, Paul Elek.

284. NICHOLSON, N. (1949*) Cumberland and Westmorland* London, Robert Hale.

285. 'Cumberland and Westmorland (County Books)' by Nicholson (author) book review by Roberts, Janet in *The Times Literary Supplement* , Friday, November 25, 1949.

286. NICHOLSON, N. (1963) *Portrait of the Lakes*, London, Robert Hale.

287. Most kindly presented to the author of this book by Mr Bernard Hamilton.

288. NICHOLSON, N. (1955) *The Lakers: The First Tourists London, Robert Hale*

289. Poem 'To The River Duddon' from Nicholson's *Five Rivers.*

290. NICHOLSON, N. (1977) *The Lake District: An Anthology London, Robert Hale.*

291. WYATT, J. (1973) *The Shining Levels: the story of a man who went back to Nature* London Geoffrey Bles.

292. London Robert Hale.

293. London Robert Hale.

294. Nicholson was both a keen supporter and a Trustee of this little gem of a theatre at Moresby, near Whitehaven, founded by local industrialist and arts patron Sir Nicholas Sekers.

295. Although the Calder Hall cooling towers are now (in 2014) dismantled, an operational gas-fired power station at the Seascale end of the same site continues to provide such steamy effusions.

296. Strictly speaking, Calder Hall was the name of the original nuclear power station only (now closed), but in practice the names Calder Hall, Windscale and Sellafield were used interchangeably when referring to the atomic plant in general.

297. Letter from Nicholson to Daniel Hay, dated 29 October 1959 (Whitehaven County Archives).

298. As of course Nicholson often did.

299. See Chapter 11.

300. In a 1970s BBC local radio interview.

301. In 1984 LWT *South Bank Show* interview.

302. Ibid.

303. GIFFORD, T. (1995) Green *Voices* Manchester University Press.

304. Ibid.

305. The Observer Review, Sunday 1 December 1981, 'Pendennis' Column ('Of Poetry and Pots', written by Nally, Michael.)

306. BARKER, G. (1954) 'Book Reviews' *The London Magazine* Volume 1, No. 7 (pages 86-93).

307. NICHOLSON, N. (1954) *The Pot Geranium* London, Faber & Faber.

308. RIDLER, A. (1954) 'Letter to Editor' *The London Magazine* Volume 1, No. 8 (page 74).

309. Perhaps a veiled allusion, too, to Barker's prolific sex life?

310. This comment made in a private email to the author, who is reluctant fully to name the Professor, lacking express permission to do so.

311. Letter to Nicholson from Rowse, dated 22 August, 1967. Manchester University John Rylands Library catalogue ref. GB 133 NCN1/1/113.

312. SIMPSON, Matt, (1995) Review of Nicholson's 'Collected Poems' *Critical Survey,* New York & Oxford, Vol. 7, No.2.

313. The Times (London), Obituary, 1 June, 1987.

314. LEAVIS, Q.D. (1968) *A Selection From Scrutiny* Cambridge University Press and LEAVIS, F.R. (1964) *The Common Pursuit* New York University Press p. 248 *et.seq*.

315. See Chapter 3.12.

316. Leavis of course was a notoriously bad-tempered and scathingly-unkind (psychopathic, almost?) critic.

317. BRITISH BROADCASTING CORPORATION (1964) *Writers on Themselves,* London, BBC Publications (page 4).

318. A subjective impression only, but nonetheless a pervasive and clear one.

319. Indeed, in 1977, when Nicholson was awarded the Queen's Gold Medal for Poetry, Betjeman was on hand to assist with the ceremonial (and with the subsequent celebrations).

320. Bunting's best-known poem, *Briggflatts* related to a Quaker Meeting House near Sedbergh, Cumbria, hence probably the magazine's incomplete grasp of the full facts about Bunting and his work.

321. Smart tweeds, cloaks and cravats were in fact Nicholson's sartorial style.

322. Letter to Nicholson, Rylands Library, (NCN/1/1/2).

323. Letter to Nicholson, Rylands Library, (NCN/1/1/13).

324. And very highly recommended, too!

325. The comment was made by Mr Nathan Richardson on 22 January 2015 in a private communication with this book's author, David Boyd.

326. NICHOLSON, N. (1958) 'No Poetry in Railways' *The Listener,* 4 December Page 922.

327. This is cited, too, in Jones' biography, but rather as evidence that Betjeman was generally unimpressed by Nicholson's poetry.

328. LYCETT-GREEN, C. (Ed.) (1994) *Letters of John Betjeman 1926-1951* London, Methuen.

329. In the issue of this newspaper dated 6 July, 1944.

330. Document Ref. GB 133 NCN1/1/52.

331. Old UK currency: 'bob' was a slang term for one shilling which was a twentieth of one pound.

332. THWAITE, A. (Ed.) (2010) *Letters to Monica,* London, Faber & Faber.

333. THWAITE, A. (Ed.) (1992) *Selected Letters of Philip Larkin: 1940-1985,* London, Faber & Faber.

334. I am indebted to Mr Nathan Richardson for unearthing these references and for kindly sharing them.

335. LEAVIS, F.R. (1964) *The Common Pursuit* New York University Press (page 251).

336. By the company E.P. Dutton.

337. LOWELL, R. (1946) 'Current Poetry Review' *The Sewanee Review* Vol. 54 No. 1 pp. 145-153.

338. Ibid.

339. Ibid.

340. MOTION, A. (1982) 'The Modest Onlooker' *Times Literary Supplement* 10 December Page 1376.

341. Ibid.

342. PITE, R. (2010) 'His Country: Hardy in the Rural' in *A Companion to Thomas Hardy* (Ed. K. Wilson) Oxford, Wiley-Blackwell.

343. Ibid.

344. Ibid. (Nicholson was in fact first brought to Prof. Pite's attention in this context by Dr David Cooper).

345. NICHOLSON, N. (1980) 'A Poet's Tribute to Margaret Cropper' *The Church Times* 10 October.

346. GIOIA, D, *The Most Unfashionable Poet Alive: Charles Causley* [online]. Available from: http://www.danagioia.net/essays/ecausley.htm . [Accessed: 1 September, 2013].

347. In Daniel Hay's Nicholson-related cuttings collection.

348. Undated, but probably late 1940s.

349. This article was in fact an abridged version of a tribute essay by NN to Young which appeared in:- CLARK, L. (Editor) (1957) *Andrew Young Prospect of a Poet,* London: Rupert Hart-Davis, pages 61 – 68

350. E.g., BBC Radio Cumbria Interviews with Nicholson.

351. Formerly Faber and Faber's distinguished Chairman, and well known to Nicholson. He remained a Senior Consultant to the firm until his death.

352. In an (as yet) unpublished paper.

353. Of course, to Nicholson that faraway country being the Palestine of the Bible.

354. *'That Exquisite Echo': Rhyme in English Poetry from the Seventeenth Century to the Present,* 12 September 2013, McDowell, S. 'Norman Nicholson: The Surprising Inevitability of Rhyme': University of Durham.

355. DONALDSON, C., MURRIETA-FLORES, P., RUPP, C.J., GREGORY, I., HARDIE. A. and RAYSON, P., (2013) *A Spatial Analysis of Norman Nicholson's Correspondence.* Paper presented at Modernist Studies Association 2013: Sussex, UK.

356. June, 1985 pages 109-114.